List of Contents

Introduction: A New Paradigm of Wealth

In the dimly lit room, cluttered with finance books and spreadsheets, John sat hunched over his computer, his eyes fixed on the glowing screen. His mind raced with numbers, investments, and the all-too-familiar feeling of financial anxiety. He had diligently adhered to the conventional course, as many do – diligent studies, securing a commendable occupation, and conscientious saving – yet, something seemed amiss.

For years, he had adhered to the principles handed down through generations. John systematically set aside his earnings into a savings account, dabbled in a select few stocks, and made regular contributions to his employer's retirement scheme. However, despite his unwavering commitment, John's financial aspirations remained like ethereal phantoms on the remote horizon. The concept of financial freedom appeared as an unattainable mirage, and his savings account provided nothing more than meager returns.

As days turned to months, and months to years, John pondered. Could there be more to wealth acquisition than the principles with which he had been inculcated? Was the course to financial security truly paved with frugality, thrift, and unremitting toil?

John's narrative is by no means unique. It is a tale shared by innumerable individuals embarking on the orthodox path to financial prosperity. The roadmap to financial success may seem transparent: diligence in employment, prudent saving, astute investing, and unwavering patience for the fruits of labor to mature. However, reality is far more intricate.

In the ensuing pages, we embark upon an expedition. Not an extraordinary odyssey as often depicted in the annals of financial literature, but rather, a pragmatic voyage to unexplored avenues and unconventional stratagems that herald a new paradigm of wealth. This journey does not involve chasing elusive shadows or delving headlong into perilous ventures, but rather, it is a journey that empowers through knowledge, fosters strategic insight, and unlocks the concealed potential within.

The term "wealth" typically conjures images of opulent lifestyles – grand automobiles, lavish vacations, and palatial estates. Yet, contemplate for a moment if you will: wealth extends beyond the mere accumulation of material possessions. It is not solely an exercise in amassing monetary assets. Authentic wealth is a multilayered concept, transcending the confines of currency.

True wealth encompasses the liberty to pursue one's passions, to enjoy cherished moments with loved ones, and to embrace life on one's own terms. It embodies the tranquility that arises from the assurance of financial stability. It confers the capacity to contribute to the welfare of one's community, advocate for cherished causes, and establish a lasting legacy.

The traditional approach to wealth acquisition frequently emphasizes the accumulation of financial resources. This perspective has its intrinsic limits. It posits that wealth is solely a financial expedition and that the present must be relinquished for the promise of an opulent future.

The expedition we embark upon questions these accepted tenets. It seeks to cultivate a life of financial prosperity and fulfillment. It asserts that wealth is not merely a terminus, but an overarching philosophy. It begins with the recognition that one's financial prosperity is not restricted to numerical figures; it is an embodiment of values, aspirations, and distinct potential.

We shall delve into methodologies that surpass conventional approaches – that transcend mere thrift, budgetary austerity, and ordinary investment techniques. These methodologies, while recognizing the value of traditional practices, are directed at harnessing the advantages of automation, skill enrichment, prudent expenditure, and the exploration of innovative streams of income.

The principles presented in this volume are founded upon practicality, corroborated by real-life experiences, and designed to furnish the reader with the capability to make judicious financial decisions. There are no vacuous assurances, no empty conjecture. This is a clarion call to action, an exhortation to cultivate a wealth of knowledge, and a guide to its implementation in one's unique circumstances.

This publication is conceived as a handbook for the creation of a more gratifying and prosperous existence. It is a navigational chart for traversing the labyrinth of personal finance with unclouded perspective and confidence. It is an invitation to challenge the status quo, to scrutinize conventional wisdom, and to redefine the route to financial success.

This volume is a platform to transcend conventional boundaries, to redefine the meaning of authentic wealth, and to equip the reader with the tools and knowledge necessary to transform aspirations into concrete accomplishments. Our joint expedition commences herein, where financial affluence is not a far-off aspiration, but an immediate actuality. It is time to adopt a new paradigm of wealth – one that positions you as the core, in command, and progressing toward enduring prosperity.

This is not a game of chance; this is a deliberate voyage toward a future of your design, and it is set in motion now.

Part 1: Understanding Wealth Disparities

Chapter 1: The Wealth Gap

1.1 Defining Wealth Disparities

Wealth disparities are a complex and pervasive issue that has far-reaching consequences in our society. Understanding the multifaceted nature of these disparities is a critical step toward addressing them. In this section, we will delve deep into the various dimensions of wealth disparities, examining their historical roots, systemic factors, and the ways in which they continue to widen in contemporary society.

The Multifaceted Nature of Wealth Disparities

Wealth disparities encompass a wide array of differences in financial well-being between individuals and groups. These disparities can manifest in numerous forms, including income inequality, disparities in asset ownership, variations in access to education and healthcare, and disparities in opportunities for economic mobility. The multifaceted nature of wealth disparities is what makes them so challenging to address comprehensively.

One aspect of wealth disparities that often receives significant attention is income inequality. It reflects the unequal distribution of earnings among individuals and households. Some earn substantial incomes, while others struggle to make ends meet. But income is just one facet of the larger picture. Wealth disparities go beyond the paychecks we receive; they extend into the assets we own and the opportunities available to us.

Another dimension of wealth disparities involves disparities in asset ownership. This includes real estate, stocks, bonds, businesses, and other assets that hold intrinsic value. The distribution of these assets is far from equal. Wealthier individuals and families have more substantial assets, allowing them to generate passive income, while those with fewer assets may find it challenging to build wealth over time.

Historical and Systemic Factors

To understand wealth disparities fully, we must acknowledge their historical roots and systemic underpinnings. These factors have contributed significantly to the enduring wealth disparities we witness today.

Historically, wealth disparities have deep-seated origins, dating back to periods of colonization, slavery, and institutional discrimination. In the United States, for instance, the legacy of slavery and segregation has had a profound impact on the economic opportunities and wealth accumulation of Black Americans. Centuries of discriminatory policies and practices have created intergenerational wealth gaps that persist to this day.

Systemic factors, including policies, practices, and structural inequalities, continue to perpetuate wealth disparities. These systemic factors can be observed in education, housing, employment, and the criminal justice system. For example, disparities in access to quality education have a long-lasting effect on future earning potential and, consequently, wealth accumulation.

Discriminatory lending practices have hindered opportunities for homeownership among marginalized groups, further exacerbating disparities in asset ownership.

The Widening Wealth Gap in Contemporary Society

Despite societal awareness of wealth disparities, the gap continues to widen in contemporary society. Various contributing factors have been at play in recent decades.

One major factor is the unequal distribution of economic gains. Technological advancements and globalization have generated substantial wealth, but a significant portion of these gains has flowed to the highest income earners. This exacerbates income inequality and further widens the wealth gap.

Additionally, access to financial opportunities and education remains uneven. Those with greater resources often have access to better financial education, investment opportunities, and financial services that can help them build wealth more effectively. Meanwhile, marginalized communities may find themselves trapped in cycles of financial insecurity due to a lack of access to these resources.

Furthermore, the cost of living in many urban areas has skyrocketed, making it increasingly difficult for individuals with lower incomes to save and invest. This results in fewer opportunities to accumulate wealth over time.

Understanding wealth disparities is not merely an academic exercise; it is an essential step in addressing one of the most pressing economic and social challenges of our time. To tackle wealth disparities effectively, we must consider the multifaceted nature of these inequalities, recognize their historical roots and systemic perpetuation, and confront the factors that continue to widen the gap in contemporary society. Our journey toward wealth equality begins with this understanding, and the road ahead requires comprehensive and actionable solutions to create a more equitable and just future for all.

1.2 Psychological and Societal Implications

Wealth disparities are not mere statistics on a balance sheet. They are the heartbeats of economies and the pulse of societies. Behind the dry data, there's a complex and often sobering narrative that unfurls when we delve into the psychological and societal implications of wealth inequality. As we journey through this exploration, we aim to shed light on the very real, human consequences of the wealth gap.

How Wealth Disparities Affect Mental Health

Money, or the lack thereof, is a constant companion in our lives. It can be a source of security, a facilitator of dreams, or an unwelcome harbinger of stress. For those on the short end of the wealth divide, it's often the latter. The mental toll of financial strain is a burden that many bear, and its implications ripple through every facet of their lives.

The psychological implications of wealth disparities are profound. Anxiety, depression, and a pervasive sense of powerlessness often shadow those struggling to make ends meet. The relentless pressure of financial instability gnaws at one's self-esteem and mental well-being. These individuals are trapped in a persistent state of financial insecurity, a condition that makes it nearly impossible to focus on personal growth and long-term goals. They're caught in a seemingly endless cycle, with no clear way out.

When individuals face an unequal distribution of wealth, it perpetuates feelings of inequity and injustice. The persistent knowledge that others possess far more resources and opportunities can lead to resentment, further intensifying the mental burden. For those struggling, the wealth gap is not an abstract concept; it's a stark reality that sows seeds of discontent and disillusionment.

Societal Consequences of Wealth Inequality
Beyond the personal realm, wealth disparities have wide-ranging societal repercussions. They contribute to a sense of division within communities and nations. When wealth is concentrated in the hands of a few, the social fabric begins to fray. Communities become polarized along economic lines, and a sense of common purpose can diminish.

One striking outcome of wealth inequality is limited social mobility. In societies where the wealth gap is vast, it becomes exceedingly difficult for individuals from lower-income backgrounds to rise above their circumstances.

Education, job opportunities, and even access to healthcare can become exclusive privileges of the affluent. This stark division often translates to a lack of upward mobility, which can perpetuate poverty for generations.

A less tangible but equally vital societal implication is the erosion of trust. Trust in institutions, government, and even in fellow citizens can deteriorate when people perceive the system as fundamentally unfair. The societal fabric frays as cynicism takes root.

Breaking the Cycle of Poverty
The cycle of poverty is a daunting trap, one that ensnares generation after generation. Breaking free from this cycle requires a multi-faceted approach that addresses both individual and systemic challenges.

1. Financial Literacy and Education:

At its core, financial literacy is the ability to understand and use various financial skills, including personal financial management, budgeting, and investing. Teaching financial literacy is not just about balancing checkbooks; it's about empowering individuals with the knowledge and skills needed to make informed financial decisions. In schools, communities, and homes, financial education can serve as the foundation for breaking the cycle of poverty.

2. Access to Quality Education:

Education is a powerful driver of economic mobility. Ensuring that every child, regardless of their background, has access to quality education is critical. This includes investments in early childhood education, improving K-12 schools in underserved communities, and making higher education more affordable.

3. Job Opportunities and Economic Policies:

Creating job opportunities and enacting economic policies that prioritize fair wages and workers' rights can mitigate the wealth gap. Fair wages and job stability are essential for individuals and families to build financial security.

4. Mentorship and Support Systems:

Mentorship and supportive networks can play a vital role in breaking the cycle of poverty. Mentors can provide guidance, encouragement, and access to opportunities that individuals might not have otherwise.

5. Philanthropy and Social Initiatives:

In an ever-evolving society, philanthropy and social initiatives are key to addressing wealth disparities. Foundations, organizations, and individuals can actively contribute to poverty-alleviation efforts, focusing on sustainable solutions and long-term impact.

As we confront the psychological and societal implications of wealth inequality, we must recognize that these challenges are not insurmountable. With collective effort and a commitment to change, we can dismantle the barriers that perpetuate the wealth gap, providing opportunities and hope for those who have long been held back. The path to a more equitable future lies in our ability to acknowledge the problem and work together toward a solution. Wealth, in all its dimensions, should be a resource that empowers and uplifts all members of society, not just a select few.

1.3 Research and Data

In our quest to understand the profound wealth disparities that exist in today's society, we embark on a journey into the realm of research and data. This segment is not about hypothetical scenarios or anecdotal accounts; it is grounded in the cold, hard facts that underline the chasm between the wealthy and the not-so-wealthy. We will delve into key findings from extensive wealth inequality studies, explore global perspectives on wealth disparities, and uncover the pivotal role of income distribution in maintaining economic stability.

Key Findings from Wealth Inequality Studies

Wealth inequality is not a new concept; it has existed in different forms throughout human history. What has changed is the level of scrutiny and research directed towards this issue. A myriad of studies, often spanning decades, have dissected the intricate fabric of wealth disparities. The findings are not only revealing but also disconcerting.

One of the critical findings is that wealth distribution is highly skewed. A relatively small percentage of the population holds a disproportionately large share of the world's wealth. To put this into perspective, a study by Credit Suisse in 2020 revealed that the top 1% of the world's population owns over 44% of the world's wealth, while the bottom 50% collectively owns less than 2% of global wealth. This colossal gap is nothing short of staggering.

The wealth disparity also highlights the concept of the wealth spiral. Those who start with more have a higher likelihood of accumulating even more, while those who start with less find it exceedingly difficult to bridge the gap. This is due to various factors, including investment opportunities, access to quality education, and the ability to take financial risks.

The impact of these disparities is far-reaching. Wealthier individuals enjoy better healthcare, access to quality education, and a level of financial security that others can only dream of. In contrast, individuals with limited resources face a constant uphill battle, struggling to meet basic needs, let alone invest and grow their wealth. Such disparities erode the foundations of an equitable society and create a host of social and economic problems.

Global Perspectives on Wealth Disparities

Wealth disparities are not confined to a single nation or region; they are a global phenomenon. While the magnitude of wealth gaps may vary from one country to another, the underlying dynamics remain consistent. This phenomenon underscores that wealth disparities are not the result of isolated events but are deeply embedded in the global economic system.

For instance, in developed nations, wealth disparities may appear more subdued, but they still exist. The distribution of wealth is seldom equitable. It is important to understand that wealth disparities aren't merely an issue of the rich versus the poor. It's about the dynamics between the rich and the middle class, and even within the middle class itself. Often, it's the middle class that bears the brunt of these disparities, struggling to maintain a semblance of financial stability in the face of rising living costs and stagnant wages.

In developing nations, wealth disparities can be stark and disturbing. The gap between the wealthy elite and the impoverished is cavernous. It is a sobering reminder that the fight against wealth inequality is not restricted by geographic borders. The global community faces a collective challenge in addressing these disparities, as their repercussions transcend national boundaries.

The Role of Income Distribution in Economic Stability

The distribution of income and wealth is intricately connected to the stability of an economy. Economic stability is not merely the absence of recessions or fluctuations; it is also about ensuring that wealth is distributed in a manner that fosters growth and security for all. When wealth disparities are extreme, they can lead to social unrest, which, in turn, can destabilize economies.

A significant factor in income distribution is wage inequality. In an economy where a few individuals earn astronomical salaries while the majority struggle to make ends meet, the economic equilibrium is disrupted. This not only threatens the well-being of a significant portion of the population but also poses a risk to the sustainability of businesses and the overall economy.

Wage inequality also has far-reaching consequences. It impacts people's access to education, healthcare, and even their ability to save for the future. A significant portion of the population may find themselves trapped in a cycle of poverty, unable to access the opportunities that could uplift them to a better economic status.

Addressing wealth and income inequality is not only a moral imperative; it is also vital for the long-term stability and prosperity of any nation. It requires a multi-faceted approach, encompassing fiscal policies, social programs, and initiatives aimed at providing equal opportunities for all.

The stark realities of wealth disparities are not mere conjecture or opinion. They are facts, supported by a wealth of research and data. These disparities are not confined by geographic borders, and they have far-reaching implications for both individuals and the overall economic stability of nations. To bridge this chasm, it is imperative that we not only understand the issues but also actively engage in the collective effort to create a fairer and more equitable future. In the chapters to come, we will explore strategies and solutions that can empower individuals to take control of their financial destinies and work towards a more equitable wealth distribution.

Chapter 2: The Psychology of Wealth

2.1 Mindset and Wealth

In the world of personal finance, few topics are as crucial as the role of mindset in determining financial success. Money, in its essence, is a tool. It can build bridges or construct barriers, foster prosperity or fuel despair, depending on how one wields it. While the technical aspects of managing money are vital, the psychological facet is equally significant. The way we think about wealth, the beliefs we hold, and the actions we take all play pivotal roles in shaping our financial reality.

The Influence of Mindset on Financial Success

The first step in our exploration of the psychology of wealth is understanding how our mindset influences our financial success. If you've ever wondered why some people manage to accumulate wealth while others perpetually struggle, the answer often lies in their mindset.

A scarcity mindset, for instance, can be a significant hindrance. People with this outlook often view wealth as finite and elusive. They may worry about running out of money or hoard resources out of fear. This mindset can lead to poor financial decisions, such as avoiding investments, excessively cutting expenses, or making impulsive purchases driven by fear.

Conversely, those with an abundance mindset see opportunities and abundance even in challenging circumstances. They understand that wealth is not a zero-sum game, and one person's gain does not equate to another's loss. Instead of fearing scarcity, they believe in their ability to create and attract wealth.

To change your mindset, start by recognizing the scarcity-oriented thoughts and beliefs you may hold. Do you often find yourself saying, "I can't afford that" or "I'll never get ahead financially"? These thoughts can become self-fulfilling prophecies.

Begin by challenging these beliefs and replacing them with empowering, abundance-oriented thoughts. Shift from "I can't afford that" to "How can I afford that?" or from "I'll never get ahead financially" to "I am capable of building wealth over time." This mental reframing can be a powerful catalyst for making better financial decisions.

Identifying and Changing Limiting Beliefs

One of the most significant roadblocks to financial success is the presence of limiting beliefs. These are deeply ingrained convictions about money, often formed during childhood and reinforced through life experiences. Limiting beliefs can include ideas such as "money is the root of all evil," "rich people are greedy," or "I'm not smart enough to invest."

Identifying these limiting beliefs is a critical first step in transforming your financial mindset. You may not even be aware of the beliefs that hold you back, but they can subtly influence your financial decisions.

Take time to reflect on your money-related beliefs. Write them down and ask yourself where these beliefs originated. Were they inherited from your family, influenced by society, or shaped by personal experiences? Once you identify them, challenge their validity. Are they rooted in fact, or are they limiting you without cause?

Let's take the belief "money is the root of all evil" as an example. While it's crucial to acknowledge that unethical actions can be driven by money, it's equally important to recognize the positive impact that money can have. Money can fund philanthropic endeavors, support families, and drive innovations that improve society. By challenging and reshaping limiting beliefs, you open the door to a more constructive relationship with money.

Changing these limiting beliefs requires self-awareness and conscious effort. Start by identifying the beliefs that might be holding you back. Challenge their validity and replace them with empowering beliefs. For example, "I'm not good with money" can become "I am capable of learning and improving my financial skills."

Cultivating a Wealth-Oriented Mindset

Cultivating a wealth-oriented mindset is about embracing the idea that wealth is attainable and within your control. It's about making proactive choices to enhance your financial well-being and believing in your ability to shape your financial future. Here are some practical strategies to foster a wealth-oriented mindset:

1. Set Clear Financial Goals: Define your financial objectives, both short-term and long-term. Whether it's buying a home, starting a business, or retiring comfortably, clear goals provide direction and motivation.

2. Create a Financial Plan: A financial plan outlines your path to achieving your goals. It includes budgeting, saving, investing, and debt management strategies tailored to your aspirations.

3. Educate Yourself: Financial literacy is a powerful tool. Invest time in learning about personal finance, investing, and wealth-building. Books, courses, and online resources are valuable sources of knowledge.

4. Surround Yourself with Positive Influences: The people you spend time with can significantly impact your mindset. Surround yourself with individuals who have a wealth-oriented perspective and can offer guidance and support.

5. Take Ownership of Your Financial Decisions: Recognize that you have the power to shape your financial reality through your choices. Take responsibility for your financial decisions, and be prepared to learn from both successes and setbacks.

6. Practice Gratitude: Appreciating what you have, no matter how much or how little, can shift your focus away from scarcity and toward abundance. Gratitude can be a powerful driver of positive financial behaviors.

7. Visualize Success: Visualization is a technique used by many successful individuals. Envision your financial goals

as already achieved. This mental practice can help reinforce your belief in your ability to attain wealth.

The psychology of wealth is a critical factor in achieving financial success. By recognizing and shifting your mindset, identifying and challenging limiting beliefs, and actively cultivating a wealth-oriented perspective, you can set the stage for making better financial decisions and moving closer to your wealth-building goals. Remember, wealth is not an abstract concept but a tangible outcome of your thoughts, beliefs, and actions.

2.2 Behavioral Finance

Money, despite its fundamentally numerical nature, often defies logic. It behaves in unpredictable ways, not because it has a mind of its own, but because the people who handle it do. This fascinating realm is known as behavioral finance, and it's where the study of human psychology meets the world of money. Understanding this field is crucial because it sheds light on the common money biases that we all possess, the emotional decision-making processes that influence our wealth, and, most importantly, the strategies to make rational financial decisions.

Understanding Common Money Biases

Our brains are hardwired with certain biases that often lead us astray in the realm of finance. It's essential to recognize these biases to navigate the world of money more effectively.

Overconfidence Bias: This bias often leads us to believe that we're better at investing or financial decision-making than we actually are. It can cause us to take excessive risks, thinking we have the Midas touch. In reality, few individuals consistently outperform the market.

Loss Aversion: The pain of losing money is more significant than the joy of gaining it. This phenomenon explains why people often hold onto losing investments for too long, hoping they'll bounce back. It's essential to cut your losses and move on.

Confirmation Bias: We tend to seek information that confirms our existing beliefs. In the financial world, this can lead to a dangerous echo chamber effect, where we only listen to sources that reinforce our existing views. Diversify your sources of information to avoid this trap.

Anchoring: We often rely too heavily on the first piece of information we receive. For instance, if a stock is initially priced high, even if it's overvalued, we might anchor to that price and think it's a good investment. Be aware of anchoring and base your decisions on thorough research.

The Impact of Emotional Decision-Making on Wealth

Emotions and money are like a volatile cocktail. Fear, greed, excitement, and panic can drive us to make irrational decisions that can have a significant impact on our financial well-being.

Fear and Panic: During market downturns, fear and panic can lead to impulsive selling. Many investors sell low, locking in losses, when the better strategy is often to stay the course or even buy more during downturns.

Greed and Overtrading: On the flip side, excessive greed can lead to overtrading, frequent buying and selling of investments. This not only incurs transaction costs but also increases the chances of poor decision-making.

Regret Aversion: Fear of regret can cause you to avoid necessary financial decisions, like rebalancing your portfolio or selling underperforming investments. You fear making the wrong choice, so you make no choice at all.

Impulse Buying and Lifestyle Inflation: Emotional spending, particularly when experiencing financial windfalls, can lead to lifestyle inflation. Suddenly, you're spending more and saving less, which can jeopardize long-term financial security.

Strategies for Making Rational Financial Decisions
To counter these biases and emotional pitfalls, here are practical strategies for making rational financial decisions:

1. Establish Clear Goals: Start by defining your financial goals. Are you saving for retirement, a house, or your child's education? Having clear objectives helps you avoid impulsive decisions that don't align with your goals.

2. Create a Budget: A well-structured budget is your financial roadmap. It helps you track expenses, plan for the future, and avoid overspending. Tools and apps can simplify the budgeting process.

3. Diversify Your Investments: Diversification, the old adage of not putting all your eggs in one basket, is key to managing risk. Spread your investments across various asset classes to reduce exposure to a single volatile asset.

4. Automate Your Savings and Investments: Automation is your ally against procrastination and impulse spending. Set up automatic transfers to your savings and investment accounts on payday. This ensures you save and invest before spending.

5. Consult a Financial Advisor: Seeking advice from a qualified financial advisor can be invaluable. They provide an objective, rational perspective and help you avoid common biases.

6. Stay Informed and Educated: Continually educate yourself about financial markets and investment strategies. By understanding the basics, you'll be better equipped to make rational decisions.

7. Develop a Long-Term Perspective: Focus on long-term goals and avoid reacting to short-term market fluctuations. Keep in mind that time in the market is more critical than timing the market.

8. Maintain Emotional Discipline: When markets fluctuate, remind yourself of your goals and your well-thought-out

strategy. Emotional discipline can be your greatest asset in the world of finance.

Behavioral finance reveals that our financial decisions are deeply influenced by our psychology. Recognizing and mitigating biases, managing emotions, and adopting rational strategies are critical to achieving financial success. By understanding the connection between the mind and money, you can position yourself for a more prosperous financial future.

2.3 Financial Education

In the way of financial success, one factor stands out as an indispensable cornerstone: financial education. The importance of financial literacy cannot be overstated. It is the keystone that upholds your financial well-being, the lantern that dispels the darkness of ignorance, and the compass that directs your path to prosperity. In this section, we delve deep into the significance of financial literacy, explore the rich arsenal of resources and tools available for improving your financial knowledge, and unveil the enduring strategy of lifelong learning as a potent catalyst for wealth building.

The Importance of Financial Literacy

Financial literacy, in its essence, is the ability to understand and manage your financial affairs competently. It encompasses a wide array of financial topics, from budgeting and investing to understanding credit and taxes. Imagine a ship's captain navigating through treacherous waters. Without the proper charts and knowledge of navigation, the ship may end up aimlessly adrift or, worse, shipwrecked. In the same vein, without financial literacy, you risk drifting through your financial life without direction, often succumbing to the perils of debt, impulsive spending, and missed opportunities for growth.

The absence of financial education can have a profound impact on your life, leading to costly mistakes and missed chances to accumulate wealth. By enhancing your financial literacy, you equip yourself with the tools to make informed decisions, avoid financial pitfalls, and secure a brighter financial future.

But what does financial literacy entail? It starts with understanding basic financial concepts, such as budgeting, saving, and investing. It extends to comprehending more complex topics like retirement planning, tax strategies, and estate planning. Ultimately, financial literacy empowers you to make informed choices regarding your money, thereby taking charge of your financial destiny.

Financial literacy is not a static concept; it evolves with your life. As your financial situation and goals change, so too should your financial knowledge. The ability to adapt to new financial challenges and opportunities is a testament to your financial literacy.

Resources and Tools for Improving Financial Knowledge

Now that we understand the importance of financial literacy, the next logical step is to explore the resources and tools available to enhance this knowledge. Fortunately, in today's digital age, we have an abundance of resources at our fingertips, ready to guide us on our journey to financial enlightenment.

1. Books: The world of finance literature is vast and diverse. From classic personal finance books to in-depth investment guides, there's a wealth of knowledge to be gained. Authors like Benjamin Graham (The Intelligent Investor), Robert Kiyosaki(Rich Dad Poor Dad), and Gerard Alto (Win like buffet) have penned books that cater to various aspects of financial literacy. Look for books that align with your financial goals and interests.

2. Online Courses: Numerous platforms offer online courses on personal finance, investing, and related topics. Websites like Coursera, edX, and Udemy provide courses from renowned universities and instructors. These courses are often self-paced, allowing you to learn at your convenience.

3. Financial News and Magazines: Staying updated on financial news is vital for making informed decisions. Publications like The Wall Street Journal, Bloomberg, and Forbes provide valuable insights into market trends, economic updates, and personal finance tips.

4. Financial Blogs and Podcasts: The internet is teeming with financial bloggers and podcasters who share their

experiences and expertise. These resources offer practical advice, real-life case studies, and discussions on a wide range of financial topics.

5. Financial Advisors: Consider consulting with a financial advisor, especially for more complex financial matters. An experienced advisor can provide tailored guidance, helping you make the best choices for your unique financial situation.

6. Online Calculators and Tools: Various online tools and calculators can simplify financial planning. They help with tasks like budgeting, retirement planning, debt repayment, and investment analysis.

7. Library Resources: Don't overlook your local library as a valuable resource for financial education. Libraries often host financial literacy workshops and provide access to a wide array of financial books and magazines.

8. Government and Nonprofit Initiatives: Many governments and nonprofit organizations offer free or low-cost financial education programs. These programs cover topics like basic budgeting, credit management, and homebuying.

9. Peer Learning: Engaging in discussions with friends, family, or online communities can be an excellent way to share knowledge, ask questions, and learn from the experiences of others.

Lifelong Learning as a Wealth-Building Strategy

As you embark on your journey to wealth, remember that financial education is not a one-time event but an ongoing process. Lifelong learning is the strategy that keeps your financial literacy sharp and relevant. The financial landscape evolves, tax laws change, and new investment opportunities arise. Your life goals also change with time. Therefore, it is paramount to keep your financial knowledge up-to-date and aligned with your current financial objectives.

To embrace lifelong learning as a wealth-building strategy, adopt the following practices:

1. Set Clear Financial Goals: Define your short-term and long-term financial goals. Your educational pursuits should align with these goals.

2. Regularly Review Your Finances: Periodically assess your financial situation and identify areas where you need to expand your knowledge. This might include improving your investment expertise, understanding tax implications, or learning about estate planning.

3. Attend Seminars and Workshops: Participate in financial seminars, workshops, and conferences. These events provide an opportunity to interact with experts, ask questions, and gain deeper insights into specific financial topics.

4. Subscribe to Quality Publications: Stay current with financial news and analysis by subscribing to reliable publications. Consider journals and magazines that focus

on your specific interests, whether it's stock market investing or real estate.

5. Network with Experts: Build relationships with financial professionals and experts in areas relevant to your financial goals. Their insights and mentorship can be invaluable.

6. Stay Inquisitive: Cultivate a curious mindset when it comes to your finances. Always be ready to ask questions and seek answers to deepen your understanding.

7. Apply Your Knowledge: The best way to solidify your financial education is by putting your knowledge into action. As you learn, apply your insights to your financial decisions and investments.

In the realm of financial education, your capacity for learning is your greatest asset. By continuously enhancing your financial literacy, you not only build wealth but also gain the confidence to navigate complex financial landscapes and make sound decisions. Consider it an ongoing journey of personal and financial growth, where knowledge becomes your most powerful tool in the pursuit of financial success.

Chapter 3: Education, Skills, and Earning Potential

3.1 The Role of Education

In the field of financial prosperity, one cannot deny the crucial role that education plays in shaping an individual's earning potential. While the relationship between education and income might seem straightforward, it's important to delve deeper into the mechanisms at play, understand the strategies for acquiring education affordably, and appreciate the ongoing journey of lifelong learning and skill development.

The Link Between Education and Earning Potential

Education is often regarded as the foundation upon which a financially secure future is built. It equips individuals with the knowledge, skills, and qualifications necessary to enter the workforce and advance their careers. In essence, education serves as a catalyst for increasing one's earning potential.

However, it's not merely about the acquisition of a degree or diploma. It's about the transformation that education brings to a person's life. When you invest in your education, you invest in yourself. It is an investment that can pay lifelong dividends in the form of higher income, job stability, and personal growth.

Strategies for Affordable and Accessible Education

The rising costs of education have made the pursuit of higher learning seem like an unattainable dream for many. However, there are strategies that can make education more affordable and accessible, even in a world where the price of knowledge seems to climb steadily.

1. Financial Aid and Scholarships: One of the most effective ways to make education affordable is by exploring financial aid and scholarships. These opportunities can significantly reduce the burden of tuition fees and make quality education more accessible. There are countless organizations, both private and public, that offer scholarships based on academic performance, financial need, or other criteria.

2. Community Colleges and Online Learning: Traditional four-year universities are not the only path to higher education. Community colleges often offer more affordable options for basic coursework, and many universities now provide online courses. These online programs not only save on tuition costs but also offer flexibility for those who need to work while studying.

3. Employer Sponsorship and Tuition Reimbursement: Many employers recognize the value of an educated workforce. They often provide sponsorship or tuition reimbursement for employees seeking to further their education. If you're already working, inquire with your employer about available educational benefits.

4. Education Tax Benefits: Governments often provide tax benefits to individuals pursuing education. Explore options

like the Lifetime Learning Credit or the American Opportunity Tax Credit to lessen the financial burden of educational expenses.

5. Budgeting and Planning: Affordability isn't just about finding external sources of funding; it's also about managing your finances wisely. Create a budget specifically for your educational expenses, including tuition, textbooks, and materials. Planning ahead ensures you're prepared for the financial commitment.

Lifelong Learning and Skill Development
While formal education is undoubtedly valuable, it's essential to recognize that learning doesn't end with a degree or diploma. The world is ever-changing, and the job market continually evolves. To remain competitive and seize new opportunities, adopting a mindset of lifelong learning is essential.

Lifelong learning is the practice of continuously developing your skills and knowledge throughout your life. It's a commitment to staying updated in your field and embracing new challenges. It's an acknowledgment that education doesn't stop when you leave the classroom but extends into every aspect of your life.

Consider the digital revolution we've witnessed in recent years. Industries have transformed, and jobs have shifted. The ability to adapt and acquire new skills has become a prized asset. Lifelong learning is about staying relevant, agile, and prepared for whatever the ever-changing job market throws at you.

Moreover, it's not just about adapting to changes. It's also about exploring your interests and passions. Lifelong learning allows you to delve into subjects that intrigue you, whether they're directly related to your career or purely for personal enrichment.

In practice, lifelong learning can take various forms:

1. Online Courses and Workshops: The internet is a treasure trove of learning opportunities. Platforms like Coursera, edX, and LinkedIn Learning offer a wide array of courses covering topics from data science to creative writing. If you want free courses you can simply go to Google Free courses. They sometimes offer free certification if you take their courses.

2. Networking and Mentoring: Learning isn't confined to books and screens. Engaging with mentors and peers in your field can provide valuable insights and guidance. Networking events, conferences, and professional associations can facilitate these connections.

3. Reading and Research: Don't underestimate the power of reading. Books, articles, and research papers are rich sources of information. Dive into publications that interest you, both in and outside your professional field.

4. Practical Application: Learning by doing is a powerful method. Take on projects or side gigs that allow you to apply your knowledge in real-life situations.

5. Soft Skills Development: In addition to technical skills, don't forget the importance of soft skills like communication, problem-solving, and leadership. Many courses and resources are available for improving these skills.

Incorporating lifelong learning into your life is a commitment that pays dividends in the form of personal growth and expanded opportunities. It's a way of future-proofing your career and ensuring you remain a valuable asset in the ever-competitive job market.

Education isn't just a stepping stone to a job; it's an investment in yourself and your future. It's a ticket to a world of opportunities and personal development. While it can be costly, there are strategies to make education more affordable and accessible, ensuring it's within reach for those willing to pursue it.

Furthermore, education doesn't end with formal degrees. Lifelong learning and skill development are essential to staying competitive and embracing new opportunities throughout your career. With the right mindset and commitment to learning, you can unlock your full potential and create a brighter financial future for yourself.

3.2 Skill Development and Specialization

In the quest for financial success and the pursuit of wealth, the value of skills cannot be overstated. Skills are the tools in your toolkit, the assets that not only enhance your career but can open doors to opportunities you might never have imagined. When we discuss skill development and specialization in the context of building wealth, we're diving into the very foundation of your earning potential.

Identifying and Developing High-Demand Skills

The first step on this path is to identify high-demand skills—those proficiencies that are sought after in the job market. These are skills that organizations are willing to pay a premium for because they solve real problems and drive value. The ever-evolving landscape of the job market and industry demands means that high-demand skills can vary over time. Therefore, staying informed and adaptable is essential.

To identify these skills, you can start by examining job postings in your field of interest or in areas with growth potential. What are the skills that companies are consistently looking for? For instance, in the tech industry, skills like coding, data analysis, and artificial intelligence have been in high demand. In healthcare, specialized skills in areas like telemedicine and medical data analysis are becoming increasingly valuable.

Once you've identified high-demand skills, it's time to embark on the journey of skill development. Whether through formal education, online courses, or mentorship, invest your time and energy in acquiring and honing these skills. This might involve acquiring relevant certifications, attending workshops, or enrolling in courses from reputable institutions. Remember, becoming proficient in high-demand skills can set you apart and enhance your earning potential substantially.

The Value of Specialization and Expertise

While high-demand skills are essential, specialization takes your earning potential to another level. It's a step beyond being competent—it's about becoming an expert in a specific niche. Specialization allows you to offer unique and in-depth solutions that few others can provide.

For example, consider the field of digital marketing. Having strong digital marketing skills is great, but specializing in a niche like search engine optimization (SEO) for e-commerce businesses can make you a sought-after expert in a specific area. Your ability to drive specific, measurable results in this niche can command higher fees and job offers.

Specialization not only provides you with a competitive edge but often leads to increased job security. In rapidly changing industries, specialists are more resilient to automation or outsourcing. Companies are willing to pay a premium for the expertise and experience of specialists because they bring a depth of knowledge that's hard to replicate.

Navigating Career Changes and Growth

Specializing in a particular skill or niche can be immensely rewarding, but it doesn't mean you're locked into one path forever. In fact, many successful individuals have leveraged their high-demand, specialized skills to navigate career changes and seize new opportunities.

The journey of skill development doesn't end with one specialization. The skills you gain along the way, like adaptability and critical thinking, serve as valuable assets in themselves. As you accumulate experience and expertise, you'll find that they can be applied to a broader range of roles and industries.

For instance, someone who specialized in data analysis may discover that their problem-solving abilities are highly transferrable. They can transition into roles that involve strategic planning, market research, or even entrepreneurship. The value of your skills transcends the specifics of your initial specialization.

In the pursuit of wealth, it's crucial to view your career as a series of stepping stones, each one building upon the last. Each skill you develop, each specialization you master, equips you with the tools to seize new opportunities and maximize your earning potential.

The journey of skill development and specialization is an investment in your earning potential. Identifying high-demand skills, specializing in a niche, and staying open to career changes are key elements of building wealth. By becoming proficient and adapting to the ever-changing demands of the job market, you position yourself for financial success and a fulfilling career.

3.3 Earning More Through Negotiation

In the quest for financial success, increasing your earning potential is often a pivotal step. You might have a solid educational background and valuable skills, but to truly maximize your income, it's essential to become adept at the art of negotiation. Salary negotiations are not just reserved for career milestones; they should be an integral part of your professional journey. This section will explore strategies for successful salary negotiations, shed light on gender and wage disparities, and provide guidance on advancing your career.

Strategies for Successful Salary Negotiations

Salary negotiations can be intimidating, but mastering this skill is an essential part of achieving your financial goals. Here's a step-by-step guide to help you negotiate effectively:

1. Do Your Homework:

Before you even step into the negotiation room, make sure you've done your homework. Research the industry standards for your position and location. Websites like Glassdoor, Payscale, and the Bureau of Labor Statistics can provide valuable salary information. Knowing the salary range for your role will give you a strong starting point.

2. Highlight Your Value:

When negotiating, it's crucial to showcase your unique value to the organization. Highlight your accomplishments, skills, and the impact you've made on the company. Discuss specific projects or achievements that demonstrate your worth. Be prepared to articulate how you've contributed to the success of your team or organization.

3. Practice Your Pitch:

Preparation is the key to a successful negotiation. Rehearse your pitch in advance. Write down your talking points and practice them with a friend or in front of a mirror. This will boost your confidence and ensure you deliver a compelling argument during the negotiation.

4. Be Confident, Not Arrogant:

Confidence is essential in negotiations, but there's a fine line between being self-assured and arrogant. Be assertive, yet respectful. Maintain eye contact and a firm handshake, and use a clear and steady tone of voice. Show that you believe in your worth and your ability to contribute.

5. Don't Be Afraid to Ask:

One of the biggest mistakes people make during negotiations is not asking for what they want. Don't be afraid to make the first move. After you've discussed your accomplishments and the value you bring to the company, clearly state your salary expectations. Remember, you're there to advocate for your interests.

6. Listen Actively:

Negotiations should be a two-way conversation. Listen carefully to what the other party has to say. Their feedback and counteroffer can provide insights into the company's position. Be open to compromise and flexible in finding a solution that works for both parties.

Gender and Wage Disparities

Unfortunately, wage disparities persist in the workforce, with women and other marginalized groups often earning less for the same work. Addressing these disparities is crucial for achieving financial success and ensuring equal pay for equal work.

Recognizing Wage Disparities:

Wage disparities are a harsh reality in many industries. Women, especially women of color, continue to earn less than their male counterparts for the same work. This wage gap is often the result of systemic biases, unequal opportunities, and a lack of transparency in compensation practices.

Why Wage Disparities Exist:

Wage disparities aren't just a statistical quirk; they have deep-seated roots. Some key factors contributing to this issue include:

1. Negotiation Disparities:

Research shows that women, on average, negotiate their salaries less often than men. When they do negotiate, they often ask for less than men. The lack of negotiation can significantly impact lifetime earnings.

2. Stereotyping and Bias:

Implicit biases can affect hiring, promotions, and salary decisions. Managers may unconsciously undervalue women's contributions or underestimate their negotiation skills.

3. Family Caregiving:

Women are often more likely to take on caregiving responsibilities, which can lead to career interruptions and reduced opportunities for advancement.

Addressing Gender Disparities:

Addressing gender disparities in earnings is a complex challenge, but several strategies can help individuals and organizations make progress:

1. Negotiation Training:

Organizations can offer negotiation training for employees to close the negotiation gap. This empowers women to advocate for their worth.

2. Pay Transparency:

Greater pay transparency can help identify wage disparities within an organization. It also encourages employers to rectify any unfair wage gaps.

3. Flexible Work Arrangements:

Offering flexible work arrangements can help balance career and caregiving responsibilities, ensuring that women are not penalized for taking on caregiving roles.

Advancing Your Career and Increasing Your Earning Potential

Negotiation isn't the only way to boost your income. Advancing your career is a more comprehensive strategy that involves continually improving your skills, increasing your visibility, and pursuing opportunities for growth.

1. Lifelong Learning:

Investing in education and skill development is a lifelong endeavor. Consider further studies, certifications, or online courses to stay current and valuable in your field.

2. Networking:

Building a strong professional network can open doors to new opportunities and mentorship. Attend industry events, connect with colleagues, and seek out mentors who can guide your career.

3. Leadership Development:

Assuming leadership roles and responsibilities can lead to higher income. Leadership positions often come with increased compensation and additional benefits.

4. Job Mobility:

Don't be afraid to explore new job opportunities. Job mobility can provide a significant income boost, especially if you leverage your skills and experience to secure a higher-paying position elsewhere.

5. Personal Branding:

Developing a personal brand can make you more marketable and attractive to employers. Use social media, professional websites, and personal projects to showcase your expertise.

In the ever-evolving world of work, your ability to earn what you deserve hinges on your negotiation skills, awareness of wage disparities, and a proactive approach to advancing your career. Remember that your income isn't just a number on a paycheck; it's a crucial element in achieving your financial goals and securing your financial future.

Part 2. The Equation of Wealth

Chapter 4: Strategies for Building Wealth

4.1 Budgeting and Saving

Budgeting and saving are the foundational building blocks of wealth creation. They're not glamorous or flashy, but they are the bedrock upon which your financial fortress stands. In this section, we'll delve into the importance of budgeting, explore effective saving strategies, and discuss the power of automating your finances for success.

The Importance of Budgeting

Budgeting often gets a bad rap. People associate it with restriction and deprivation. But, in reality, a budget is your financial GPS. It's not about saying "no" to everything; it's about saying "yes" to the things that matter most.

A budget provides you with a clear picture of where your money is going. It's a map that shows you how to reach your financial goals. You begin by tracking your income and expenses, categorizing your spending, and identifying areas where you can make adjustments.

Budgeting serves several vital purposes:

1. Financial Clarity: A budget reveals your financial reality. It helps you understand where your money is flowing, uncovering any leaks or opportunities for improvement.

2. Goal Alignment: It allows you to allocate your resources toward what's important to you. Want to save for a dream vacation, a new home, or early retirement? A budget helps you direct your funds accordingly.

3. Debt Management: If you're grappling with debt, a budget provides a framework for debt reduction. It helps you allocate extra funds toward paying down high-interest debts.

4. Emergency Preparedness: Budgeting helps you build an emergency fund, providing a financial safety net for unexpected expenses.

5. Peace of Mind: Knowing where your money is going reduces financial stress. You have a plan in place, which can be incredibly reassuring.

Effective Saving Strategies
Saving is a fundamental component of wealth accumulation. It's the part of your budget dedicated to securing your financial future. Effective saving is not merely stashing money under your mattress; it's about making your money work for you.

1. Pay Yourself First: This principle is simple but profound. When you receive your income, the first bill you pay is to yourself. Automate your savings by having a portion of your paycheck automatically deposited into a dedicated savings account or investment vehicle.

2. Set Specific Goals: Saving without a goal can feel aimless. Do you want to save for a down payment on a home, a child's education, or retirement? Having specific objectives gives your savings purpose.

3. Create a Separate Savings Account: Consider opening a separate savings account, different from your checking account, to reduce the temptation to dip into your savings for daily expenses.

4. Use Windfalls Wisely: Windfalls, such as tax refunds or work bonuses, can be a substantial boost to your savings. Allocate a portion of these unexpected funds to your savings goals.

5. Consistency is Key: Saving regularly, even if it's a small amount, adds up over time. It's the habit of saving that matters more than the initial amount.

6. Emergency Fund: Build an emergency fund equivalent to 3-6 months' worth of living expenses. It provides financial security and prevents you from turning to high-interest debt in case of unforeseen events.

Automating Your Finances for Success

Automation is a powerful wealth-building tool. It ensures that your financial goals are met consistently and reduces the chances of impulsive or emotional spending decisions.

1. Automatic Transfers: Set up automatic transfers from your checking account to your savings or investment accounts. When your paycheck arrives, a portion is automatically funneled into savings before you can spend it elsewhere.

2. Bill Payments: Automate your bill payments to ensure you never miss a due date, which can lead to late fees or damage your credit score.

3. Retirement Contributions: If your employer offers a retirement plan, like a 401(k), sign up for automatic contributions. These contributions are often pre-tax, reducing your taxable income.

4. Debt Repayment: Automate minimum payments on your debts to avoid late fees and maintain a positive credit history.

5. Review and Adjust: While automation is powerful, it's not set-it-and-forget-it. Regularly review your automated processes to ensure they align with your current financial goals and circumstances.

Budgeting, saving, and automating your finances are the pillars of wealth creation. They set the stage for more advanced investment strategies and financial growth. By creating a budget, saving consistently, and automating your financial actions, you take charge of your financial future and pave the way for achieving your wealth-building goals. It may not be the most exciting part of the financial world, but it's the steady and determined road to financial success.

4.2 Investment Basics

In the world of wealth-building, understanding investment basics is akin to mastering the keys to the financial kingdom. It's the art of turning your hard-earned money into a wellspring of future prosperity. But before we dive into the specifics, let's remember one key principle: investing isn't about getting rich quickly; it's about growing your wealth steadily over time. So, let's explore the fundamental building blocks of investment basics.

Different Investment Options and Their Risk Levels

Investing is a realm brimming with options. Each comes with its own potential rewards and risks. To make informed choices, it's vital to grasp the range of investment vehicles available.

1. Stocks: Investing in stocks means becoming a shareholder in a company. It offers the potential for high returns but also carries the highest risk. Stock values can fluctuate wildly, reflecting market sentiment, economic conditions, and company performance. Consider stocks for long-term growth but be ready for market ups and downs.

2. Bonds: Bonds are essentially loans you give to governments or corporations. In return, you receive periodic interest payments, plus the principal amount upon maturity. Bonds are generally less volatile than stocks but provide lower returns. They are often used to balance risk in an investment portfolio.

3. Real Estate: Real estate investments can range from physical property ownership to Real Estate Investment Trusts (REITs) and real estate crowdfunding. Real estate offers potential rental income and property appreciation. It

tends to be less liquid but provides diversification and stability to a portfolio.

4. Mutual Funds: Mutual funds pool money from various investors to invest in a diversified portfolio of stocks, bonds, or other assets. They're managed by professionals and offer diversification and ease of access. However, fees and expenses can impact returns.

5. Exchange-Traded Funds (ETFs): ETFs are similar to mutual funds but trade on stock exchanges like individual stocks. They offer diversification, low expense ratios, and liquidity.

6. Commodities: Commodities include physical goods like gold, oil, or agricultural products. Investing in commodities can act as a hedge against inflation, but they can be volatile and may require specialized knowledge.

7. Options and Derivatives: These are advanced investment strategies that involve contracts rather than owning the underlying asset. They can be highly complex and speculative, making them suitable for experienced investors.

8. Cryptocurrencies: Digital currencies like Bitcoin have gained popularity as alternative investments. They are highly volatile and speculative, so approach them with caution and a willingness to do thorough research.

Understanding the risk associated with each investment type is critical. Generally, investments with higher potential returns often come with higher risk. Diversification, which we'll discuss shortly, can help manage this risk.

Creating an Investment Portfolio

Building a strong investment portfolio is like constructing a sturdy financial house. It's all about balance and diversification. Here's a breakdown of the key elements:

1. Asset Allocation: Determine how to distribute your investments among different asset classes. The right mix of stocks, bonds, real estate, and other assets depends on your financial goals, risk tolerance, and time horizon. For instance, a young investor with a long time horizon may opt for a more stock-heavy allocation, while someone approaching retirement might favor bonds and more conservative options.

2. Risk Tolerance: Understand your risk tolerance – how much market volatility you can stomach. Your risk tolerance should align with your financial goals and timeline. It's crucial to balance the potential for high returns with your ability to withstand losses without losing sleep.

3. Diversification: Diversifying your portfolio involves spreading your investments across a variety of assets. This strategy helps reduce the risk associated with any single investment. When one asset class underperforms, others may pick up the slack. Think of it as the financial equivalent of not putting all your eggs in one basket.

4. Regular Contributions: Consistency is the name of the game. Regularly adding money to your investment accounts, such as your 401(k) or IRA, allows you to benefit from dollar-cost averaging. This means you buy more shares when prices are low and fewer when prices are high, smoothing out market volatility.

5. Rebalancing: Periodically review your portfolio to ensure it stays in line with your target asset allocation. Rebalancing involves buying or selling assets to restore the desired allocation. It prevents your portfolio from becoming too risky or too conservative as market conditions change.

Now, let's delve into the concept of diversification as a risk management strategy.

Diversification as a Risk Management Strategy

Diversification is the financial equivalent of having a safety net beneath your high-wire act. It's a risk management strategy that helps spread your investments across a range of asset classes, reducing the impact of a single investment's poor performance on your overall portfolio.

Here's how diversification works:

- Asset Classes: Diversify across different asset classes, such as stocks, bonds, and real estate. These classes tend to perform differently under various economic conditions. When one class is down, another may be up.

- Geography: Consider investments in both domestic and international markets. International investments can provide exposure to different economic cycles and opportunities.

- Sectors: Within the stock market, diversify across various sectors like technology, healthcare, finance, and consumer goods. Each sector can perform differently based on market conditions.

- Individual Securities: If you're investing in stocks, diversify by investing in a variety of companies across different industries. This reduces the risk associated with the potential underperformance of a single company.

- Investment Vehicles: Utilize a mix of investment vehicles like mutual funds, ETFs, and individual stocks to achieve diversification within each asset class.

Diversification aims to balance risk and return. While it doesn't eliminate risk entirely, it's a powerful tool for managing it. By diversifying your investments, you can spread the risk across a broader spectrum, making it less likely that a single investment's poor performance will derail your financial goals.

To sum it up, investing is a disciplined journey toward financial goals. It's about understanding the fundamentals of different investment options, creating a well-structured portfolio, and strategically diversifying to manage risk. This roadmap, combined with a long-term perspective and consistent contributions, can set you on the path to financial success.

4.3 Entrepreneurship and Innovation

In the world of wealth creation, entrepreneurship and innovation are like two sides of the same coin. Both demand vision, determination, and an unwavering commitment to carving a path toward financial success. Whether you're just starting your journey toward financial prosperity or looking to enhance your existing wealth, understanding the entrepreneurial mindset, mastering the art of innovation, and taking strategic steps to launch and grow your business are crucial elements on your road to riches.

The Entrepreneurial Mindset and Traits

The entrepreneurial journey begins in the mind. It's a realm where ideas are hatched, risks are contemplated, and the fervor of adventure resides. An entrepreneurial mindset is marked by a unique set of traits that distinguish it from other walks of life.

1. Visionary Perspective:

Entrepreneurs have a knack for seeing opportunities where others see obstacles. They can identify gaps in the market and visualize solutions before anyone else. This vision is the foundation of their endeavors.

2. Risk Tolerance:

Risk is the faithful companion of entrepreneurship. Entrepreneurs are no strangers to calculated risks. They understand that to reap substantial rewards, they must occasionally step into the unknown.

3. Tenacity:

Entrepreneurs possess an unshakable resolve. When faced with adversity, they don't crumble; they adapt and find new ways to overcome challenges. Their perseverance is the driving force behind their success.

4. Adaptability:

In the rapidly changing landscape of business, adaptability is a prized trait. Entrepreneurs can pivot, reinvent, and transform their strategies as circumstances evolve.

5. Leadership Skills:

Entrepreneurs are often at the helm of their businesses. They must inspire and lead their teams to success, even in the face of uncertainty.

Steps to Start and Grow a Successful Business

Turning entrepreneurial aspirations into a thriving business requires careful planning and strategic execution. Here are the critical steps to follow:

1. Idea Generation:

The foundation of any business is an innovative idea. Seek opportunities within your areas of expertise, passions, and the problems you're genuinely interested in solving. Ask yourself: What issues need solutions, and can I provide them?

2. Market Research:

Once you have a business concept, delve into market research. Study your target audience, competition, and industry trends. Identify gaps and opportunities that your business can exploit.

3. Business Plan:

Create a comprehensive business plan outlining your goals, strategies, revenue models, and financial projections. A well-structured plan serves as your roadmap and can be a valuable asset when seeking funding.

4. Funding and Resources:

Most businesses require capital to get off the ground. Consider various sources of funding, from personal savings and loans to venture capital and angel investors. Secure the resources necessary to kickstart your venture.

5. Legalities and Registration:

Ensure your business complies with all legal requirements. Register your business, obtain necessary licenses, and adhere to regulations. Seek legal counsel if needed.

6. Branding and Marketing:

Develop a strong brand identity and marketing strategy. Effective branding and marketing are essential for attracting customers and establishing your business in the market.

7. Execution and Adaptation:

Start your business and execute your plan diligently. Be prepared to adapt as you gain insights into customer behavior and market dynamics.

8. Scaling and Growth:

As your business succeeds, consider opportunities for growth and scaling. This might involve expanding product lines, reaching new markets, or franchising.

The Role of Innovation in Wealth Creation
Innovation is the driving force behind many successful businesses. It's about identifying novel approaches,

processes, and products that stand out in the market. Here's how innovation plays a pivotal role in wealth creation:

1. Competitive Advantage:

Innovation provides a competitive edge. Unique products or services, efficient processes, or groundbreaking marketing strategies set your business apart from the competition.

2. Problem Solving:

Innovation thrives when addressing challenges. Entrepreneurs often seek to solve pressing problems in creative ways. The more significant the issue you address, the greater your potential for wealth creation.

3. Market Leadership:

Innovators often become market leaders. Being at the forefront of an industry allows you to set prices, influence trends, and, ultimately, reap the rewards of your ingenuity.

4. Wealth Generation:

Innovation is intrinsically tied to wealth creation. New ideas lead to novel revenue streams. Entrepreneurs who innovate successfully can capture significant market share and, consequently, substantial profits.

5. Sustained Growth:

Innovation isn't a one-time event; it's an ongoing process. It fuels sustained growth, ensuring that your business remains relevant and prosperous over time.

Bringing It All Together

The path to wealth creation is intricate, but entrepreneurship and innovation form essential pillars of that journey. Entrepreneurs exhibit a unique mindset and a set of traits that drive them to seek opportunities, take calculated risks, and persevere through adversity. They're visionaries who embrace change and create solutions to problems. The entrepreneurial journey begins with an idea and is guided by a well-thought-out business plan. It requires adaptability, leadership skills, and a deep understanding of the market.

Innovation is the linchpin of wealth creation in the business world. It sets you apart from competitors, allows you to address significant challenges, and positions you as a leader in your field. Innovative thinking and problem-solving lead to sustained growth and the generation of substantial wealth.

Together, entrepreneurship and innovation can catalyze your financial success. The key is to embrace the entrepreneurial mindset, take strategic steps to start and grow your business, and prioritize innovation in your endeavors. As you embark on this journey, remember that the road to wealth creation is filled with challenges and opportunities. Stay adaptable, be persistent, and continue learning and innovating. With determination and the right strategies, you can create a path to financial prosperity that's uniquely yours.

4.4 Financial Independence and Early Retirement

Financial independence is not a distant dream but an achievable goal for those who are willing to embrace a well-defined strategy and financial discipline. In recent years, the concept of Financial Independence, Retire Early (FIRE) has gained popularity. FIRE is a movement that revolves around the idea of achieving financial freedom and retiring earlier than the traditional retirement age, often in one's 40s or even earlier. This section will delve into the concept of financial independence, strategies for achieving early retirement, and the essence of living a fulfilling life in retirement.

The Concept of Financial Independence (FIRE)

Financial independence is the state where your investments and passive income sources generate enough money to cover your living expenses. It liberates you from the necessity of working to make ends meet. The FIRE movement is founded on several key principles:

1. Aggressive Saving: FIRE enthusiasts adopt a frugal lifestyle and save a significant portion of their income, often 50% or more. This relentless saving sets the foundation for financial independence.

2. Smart Investing: Investing is a core component of FIRE. Those seeking financial independence make well-informed investment choices to grow their wealth over time. Common investment options include low-cost index funds, dividend-paying stocks, and real estate.

3. Expense Management: FIRE adherents meticulously track their expenses and trim unnecessary spending. This careful scrutiny of expenditures helps in optimizing savings and investments.

4. Debt Elimination: Reducing and eliminating high-interest debt is a priority. Achieving financial independence becomes easier when you're not weighed down by debt payments.

5. Retirement Withdrawal Rate: The 4% rule is a common guideline in the FIRE community. It suggests that you can withdraw 4% of your portfolio annually in retirement without depleting your savings. This principle aids in calculating how much you need to accumulate to retire early.

Strategies for Achieving Early Retirement

1. Define Your FIRE Number: To achieve early retirement, you must determine your FIRE number, which represents the amount of savings required to support your desired lifestyle. This involves calculating your annual expenses and multiplying them by 25 (based on the 4% rule). For example, if your annual expenses are $40,000, your FIRE number would be $1 million.

2. Aggressive Saving and Investing: As mentioned earlier, saving a significant portion of your income is crucial. Look for ways to increase your savings rate, such as cutting unnecessary expenses and finding additional income sources. Invest wisely, considering a diversified portfolio that aligns with your risk tolerance and financial goals.

3. Maximize Tax-Advantaged Accounts: Take full advantage of retirement accounts like a 401(k) or an Individual Retirement Account (IRA). Contributions to these accounts can provide tax benefits and compound over time.

4. Side Hustles and Passive Income: Consider creating multiple income streams through side businesses or investments. Passive income sources like dividends, rental income, or royalties can significantly contribute to your early retirement journey.

5. Healthcare and Contingency Planning: Early retirees need to plan for healthcare coverage until they're eligible for Medicare. Ensure you have a safety net to handle unexpected expenses, like medical emergencies or economic downturns.

Living a Fulfilling Life in Retirement

Achieving financial independence and early retirement is a significant accomplishment, but it's essential to think beyond the financial aspects. Living a fulfilling life in retirement means considering other dimensions:

1. Purpose and Passion: Early retirement provides the opportunity to explore your passions and interests. It's a time to find a sense of purpose beyond the daily grind.

2. Health and Well-Being: Prioritize physical and mental health. Staying active, maintaining a balanced diet, and nurturing relationships are vital for a satisfying retirement.

3. Community and Social Connections: Engage with your community, make new friends, and maintain existing relationships. Building a social network in retirement can bring joy and support.

4. Continued Learning: Retirement doesn't mean stopping personal growth. Pursue lifelong learning, take up new hobbies, or even consider part-time work that aligns with your interests.

5. Travel and Experiences: If travel is your passion, early retirement can provide the freedom to explore the world. Plan and budget for experiences that bring you joy and fulfillment.

6. Volunteer and Give Back: Consider giving back to society through volunteer work or charitable endeavors. Many retirees find immense fulfillment in helping others.

The FIRE movement offers a strategic approach to financial independence and early retirement. It's about saving, investing, and living intentionally to create a life that's not solely focused on work but on what truly matters to you. While achieving early retirement is challenging, it can be a highly rewarding journey that opens up a world of opportunities for a fulfilling and purpose-driven life in your post-work years. By understanding the concept of financial independence and implementing the strategies mentioned, you can take steps toward making your early retirement dreams a reality.

4.5 Building Multiple Streams of Income

In the relentless pursuit of financial security and long-term wealth-building, the concept of having multiple streams of income stands as a pillar of strength. It's not a mere suggestion but a financial necessity. Relying solely on a traditional 9-to-5 job is like building a house on a single pillar; it might suffice for a while, but it's hardly a resilient structure when the storms of life hit.

This section explores the essence of diversifying income sources, embracing passive income streams, and tapping into the transformative power of side hustles and freelancing. These strategies are like building additional support beams for your financial house, ensuring it can withstand the uncertainties of the modern world.

Diversifying Income Sources for Financial Security

Diversification is not a term exclusive to investment portfolios. It applies to your income sources as well. While your primary job provides the foundation of your earnings, it's vital to explore alternative sources that can supplement and safeguard your financial stability. This diversification can include:

1. Investments: Beyond traditional savings accounts, explore investments like stocks, bonds, real estate, and mutual funds. By putting your money to work, you can generate additional income and potentially see it grow over time.

2. Rental Income: Owning and renting out property, be it residential or commercial, can serve as a steady stream of income. It's an investment that can yield monthly returns while potentially appreciating in value.

3. Dividends and Interest: Consider investments in dividend-paying stocks and interest-bearing bonds. These can provide periodic payouts, adding to your income without you lifting a finger.

4. Passive Income Streams: Passive income streams are a testament to the modern age. These sources include royalties, income from online businesses, and other ventures that require initial effort but yield ongoing returns.

Passive Income Streams and Investments

Passive income streams are the foundation of financial independence. These are the earnings that flow in with minimal effort on your part once the initial work is done. Such streams might include:

1. Royalties: If you possess intellectual property, like a book, music, or software, royalties from licensing can provide continuous income. For instance, a well-written book can continue to generate income long after its initial release.

2. Dividend Stocks: Investing in dividend-paying stocks can be a reliable source of passive income. Many established companies share a portion of their profits with stockholders through dividends.

3. Peer-to-Peer Lending: In the digital era, you can become a lender through peer-to-peer lending platforms. These provide an opportunity to earn interest on money lent to individuals or small businesses.

4. Real Estate Crowdfunding: Real estate crowdfunding platforms allow you to invest in real estate projects with a relatively low initial capital. You can receive a share of the rental income and potential profits from property sales.

5. Online Businesses: Building an online business, such as a blog, YouTube channel, or e-commerce store, can generate income through advertising, sponsorships, and product sales.

The Power of Side Hustles and Freelancing

In the age of the gig economy, side hustles and freelancing are not mere trends but powerful financial tools. They offer several advantages:

1. Additional Income: A well-planned side hustle or freelancing gig can provide an immediate boost to your income. It's a path to augment your earnings while keeping your primary job.

2. Flexibility: Side hustles and freelancing offer the freedom to work when and where you want. This flexibility enables you to control your workload and maintain work-life balance.

3. Skill Development: Many side hustles and freelance work offer the opportunity to enhance your skill set. You can learn new skills or leverage existing ones to generate income.

4. Entrepreneurship: For those with an entrepreneurial spirit, side hustles can be a stepping stone to starting your own business. It's a low-risk way to test your business idea and build a client base.

5. Risk Mitigation: By diversifying your income with side hustles or freelancing, you become less vulnerable to job loss or economic downturns. It's a proactive approach to securing your financial future.

Building Multiple Streams of Income: A Real-Life Strategy

To illustrate the power of diversifying income, let's consider the case of Jane, a 30-year-old marketing professional who earns a comfortable salary but aspires to build multiple income streams:

1. Investments: Jane allocates a portion of her savings into a diversified investment portfolio. She focuses on low-cost index funds and dividend-paying stocks, which gradually generate additional income over time.

2. Rental Income: With her stable job and some savings, Jane invests in a rental property. The rental income supplements her salary and offers the potential for property appreciation.

3. Passive Income Streams: Inspired by her creative side, Jane self-publishes a book on marketing strategies. As the book gains traction, she enjoys continuous royalties from sales. Additionally, she starts an affiliate marketing website, promoting products relevant to her field, generating passive income from commissions.

4. Side Hustles: Jane's love for photography leads her to start a side gig as a portrait photographer on weekends. This not only boosts her income but also provides opportunities to expand her photography skills. She also offers marketing consulting services on a freelance basis, capitalizing on her expertise.

Jane's strategy involves continuous learning, investing her time and skills in ventures that align with her interests and financial goals. With time, her diversified income sources contribute significantly to her financial security, making her less dependent on her primary job.

Building multiple streams of income is a potent strategy for enhancing your financial stability and achieving long-term wealth. It involves smart investing, passive income streams, and the pursuit of side hustles and freelancing. While it requires effort and planning, the potential rewards in terms of financial security and independence make it a path worth considering.

Chapter 5: Risk Management and Financial Security

5.1 Understanding Risk and Reward

When it comes to the realm of finance, understanding the concept of risk and reward is akin to navigating a complex puzzle. It is a critical cornerstone of investment decisions and, if mastered, can unlock a world of wealth-building opportunities. In this section, we will delve deep into the intricacies of risk and reward, emphasizing the principles of the risk-return tradeoff, assessing your risk tolerance, and ultimately achieving a balance that leads to financial security.

The Risk-Return Tradeoff in Investments

One of the fundamental principles of investing is the risk-return tradeoff. It's a simple concept with profound implications. In essence, it suggests that the potential return on an investment is directly related to the level of risk associated with it. The higher the expected return, the greater the risk.

Imagine you have two investment opportunities: the first offers a guaranteed return of 2% annually, while the second promises an average annual return of 10%. At first glance, the second option appears more lucrative, but there's a catch. The higher potential return is coupled with a higher level of risk, which means your investment could experience significant fluctuations or even losses.

This tradeoff is at the core of investment decision-making. It forces investors to weigh the potential for higher returns against the possibility of losing a portion of their investment. The key to navigating this tradeoff is aligning your investment choices with your risk tolerance and financial goals.

Assessing Your Risk Tolerance

Risk tolerance is a deeply personal aspect of investing. It's influenced by factors like your financial goals, time horizon, and emotional capacity to withstand market volatility. Assessing your risk tolerance is a crucial step in crafting an investment strategy that aligns with your unique circumstances.

To assess your risk tolerance, consider the following factors:

1. Financial Goals: Begin by clearly defining your financial goals. Are you investing for retirement, buying a home, or funding your child's education? The nature of your goals will influence your risk tolerance.

2. Time Horizon: The length of time you intend to invest is a key determinant. Longer investment horizons generally permit a higher risk tolerance, as you have more time to ride out market fluctuations.

3. Emotional Preparedness: Reflect on your emotional response to market downturns. Are you able to stay calm during market turbulence, or do you find yourself losing

sleep over financial setbacks? Emotional stability is a vital aspect of risk tolerance.

4. Risk Capacity: Consider your financial situation. How much can you afford to lose without jeopardizing your financial well-being? A solid understanding of your risk capacity ensures you don't take excessive risks.

5. Diversification: A well-diversified portfolio can mitigate risk. Assess your ability and willingness to diversify your investments across various asset classes, such as stocks, bonds, and real estate.

Once you've evaluated these factors, you'll have a clearer picture of your risk tolerance. Remember that risk tolerance is not static; it can evolve with changing life circumstances. Regularly reassess your risk tolerance to ensure your investments remain in alignment with your goals.

Balancing Risk for Financial Security

Finding the right balance between risk and security is akin to walking a tightrope. On one hand, you want your investments to generate returns that outpace inflation and work toward your financial goals. On the other, you desire a sense of financial security and peace of mind.

The key to achieving this balance lies in constructing a well-diversified portfolio. Diversification is a risk management strategy that involves spreading your investments across various asset classes and sectors. It's the financial equivalent of the age-old wisdom: "Don't put all your eggs in one basket."

Diversification is a practical approach to mitigating risk. It reduces the impact of a poor-performing investment on your overall portfolio. For instance, if you own a mix of stocks, bonds, and real estate, a significant loss in one asset class can be offset by gains in another.

Additionally, diversification helps maintain a steady growth trajectory while dampening the volatility associated with riskier assets. It's an effective way to balance the pursuit of returns with the preservation of capital.

However, striking the right balance for financial security is an ongoing process. As your financial goals evolve and market conditions change, your portfolio's composition may need adjustment. Regularly reviewing and rebalancing your investments can help you stay on track.

The understanding of the risk-return tradeoff, assessment of risk tolerance, and the pursuit of balance between risk and security are pivotal elements of sound financial decision-making. By acknowledging that risk is an inherent part of investing and learning to manage it, you can navigate the investment landscape with confidence and work towards a financially secure future.

5.2 Diversification and Asset Allocation

Investing your money can be an exciting endeavor. There's the promise of potential financial growth and the allure of watching your wealth multiply. However, the world of investing is a complex one, filled with options, risks, and strategies. In this section, we'll delve into the importance of diversification and asset allocation, two fundamental components of a sound investment strategy. These concepts might sound technical, but they're at the core of what separates successful investors from the rest.

Strategies for Diversifying Your Investment Portfolio

Diversification is akin to the wisdom of not putting all your eggs in one basket. It's a strategy that mitigates risk by spreading your investments across a range of assets. The idea is simple: if one asset performs poorly, the others can potentially balance the losses.

Imagine you have $10,000 to invest. You could put all your money into a single stock, Company XYZ. If XYZ performs well, you might see significant returns. But what if it doesn't? What if, for some unforeseen reason, its stock price plummets? Suddenly, you've lost a substantial chunk of your investment.

On the other hand, consider diversification. Instead of putting all your money into one stock, you decide to invest in a mix of stocks, bonds, real estate, and possibly even some alternative investments. This strategy helps spread the risk, so if one asset underperforms, it doesn't sink your entire portfolio. It's a bit like creating a financial safety net for your investments.

But diversification isn't just about randomly choosing assets. It's about finding the right balance and mix that suits your financial goals and risk tolerance. Your investment portfolio should align with your unique circumstances and objectives, such as saving for retirement, a house down payment, or a child's education.

The Importance of Asset Allocation

Diversification extends beyond merely investing in various asset classes. Asset allocation is the art of determining the right mix of those asset classes. Think of it as crafting a recipe with the perfect blend of ingredients. The ingredients here are the asset classes - stocks, bonds, real estate, and more.

Your choice of asset allocation largely depends on your investment horizon and risk tolerance. If you're young and aiming for long-term growth, you might opt for a more aggressive asset allocation, which includes a higher proportion of stocks. Stocks tend to offer higher returns over the long term, but they can be volatile in the short term.

On the other hand, if you're nearing retirement and prioritizing capital preservation, your asset allocation might lean more toward bonds and stable investments. Bonds are generally less risky than stocks and can provide regular income.

Here's where it gets personal. Your asset allocation isn't universal; it's tailored to you. It reflects your comfort with risk and aligns with your financial objectives. While there are conventional guidelines, like the "100 minus your age" rule (subtract your age from 100 to determine the percentage of your portfolio that should be in stocks), it's only a starting point. In reality, the right asset allocation depends on your specific circumstances, goals, and preferences.

Reducing Risk Through Smart Investment Choices

Now, let's talk about how diversification and asset allocation work together to reduce risk. The essence of this strategy is that different asset classes don't always move in sync with each other. When one asset class experiences a downturn, another might be on the upswing.

Consider this example: during a recession, stock prices may plummet due to economic uncertainty. At the same time, government bonds, seen as safer investments, often become more attractive, leading to a rise in their prices. This means that by holding both stocks and bonds in your portfolio, you can offset the losses in one asset class with gains in another.

So, how can you put these ideas into practice? Here are some strategies for diversifying your investment portfolio:

1. Spread Your Investments Across Asset Classes:

The first step to diversification is to ensure you have investments in different asset classes. This means not just focusing on stocks or bonds exclusively. By allocating your money across various categories, you reduce the risk associated with a single asset class.

2. Diversify Within Asset Classes:

Within each asset class, there's room for further diversification. For example, within the equity category, you can invest in large-cap, mid-cap, and small-cap stocks. You can also diversify by industry, geography, and style. This ensures that your investments are not overly concentrated in one area.

3. Consider Alternative Investments:

Beyond traditional stocks and bonds, there are alternative investments like real estate, commodities, and private equity. These can further enhance diversification. However, they often come with higher complexity and risk, so they should be chosen carefully.

4. Regularly Rebalance Your Portfolio:

Your asset allocation can drift over time due to the varying performance of different investments. Periodically rebalance your portfolio to maintain your desired asset mix. If one asset class becomes overweight, sell some of it and reinvest in underrepresented classes.

5. Assess Risk Tolerance and Investment Horizon:

Your asset allocation should reflect your risk tolerance and investment horizon. If you're young and have a long time horizon, you can afford to have a higher proportion of equities. If you're closer to retirement or have a lower risk tolerance, you might lean more towards bonds and cash.

Diversification and asset allocation are not one-size-fits-all solutions. Your unique financial situation and objectives will dictate the best mix for you. It's essential to revisit your portfolio regularly and make adjustments as necessary, especially as your life circumstances change.

By spreading your investments across various asset classes and regularly rebalancing your portfolio, you can minimize the impact of market volatility and work towards your long-term financial goals. While diversification doesn't guarantee a profit, it is a proven strategy to protect your investments and potentially enhance your returns over time.

5.3 Insurance and Contingency Planning

When it comes to building wealth and securing your financial future, managing risk is a cornerstone of your strategy. While you can't predict or prevent every unexpected turn of events, you can certainly prepare for them. In this section, we'll delve into the critical aspects of insurance and contingency planning, covering types of insurance, the role they play in your financial security, the importance of emergency funds, and how to mitigate the impact of unexpected financial challenges.

Types of Insurance and Their Role in Financial Security

Insurance is like a financial safety net that protects you and your assets in times of need. It comes in various forms, each serving a specific purpose in safeguarding your financial well-being. Here are some key types of insurance and their roles:

1. Health Insurance: Your health is your most valuable asset. Health insurance provides coverage for medical expenses, ensuring that you have access to necessary healthcare without depleting your savings. It's a fundamental aspect of financial security because unexpected medical bills can quickly erode your wealth.

2. Life Insurance: Life insurance is about protecting your loved ones financially in the event of your passing. It can help cover funeral expenses, pay off debts, and provide financial support to your family. While life insurance is less about you and more about your beneficiaries, it's a crucial component of a comprehensive financial plan.

3. Auto Insurance: If you own a vehicle, auto insurance is not just a legal requirement but also a financial safeguard. It covers the cost of repairs or replacements in case of accidents, and liability coverage can protect your assets if you're at fault in a collision.

4. Homeowners or Renters Insurance: This type of insurance covers your home or rental property, as well as your personal belongings inside. It's essential for protecting your dwelling and possessions from unexpected events like fires, theft, or natural disasters.

5. Disability Insurance: While we often consider life insurance, disability insurance is equally critical. It replaces a portion of your income if you're unable to work due to illness or injury. It ensures that you can continue to meet your financial obligations, even if you're temporarily unable to work.

6. Liability Insurance: Liability insurance is designed to protect you from potential legal claims. For instance, in the event of an accident on your property or a lawsuit related to your business, liability insurance can cover legal costs and potential settlements.

The role of these insurance types in financial security is clear: they provide a safety net that shields you from the financial consequences of unforeseen events. By paying a regular premium, you transfer the risk to an insurance company, allowing you to focus on building and preserving your wealth without constant worry about unexpected expenses.

Emergency Funds and Contingency Planning

While insurance is your primary defense against large, unexpected financial setbacks, you also need a personal buffer for smaller, immediate needs. This buffer comes in the form of an emergency fund, and it's an integral part of financial security.

An emergency fund is a pool of cash set aside specifically for unforeseen expenses. It provides liquidity and immediate access to funds when you need them the most. Here's how to build and manage your emergency fund:

1. Determine the Right Size: Financial experts recommend having three to six months' worth of living expenses in your emergency fund. Calculate your monthly expenditures and set a goal accordingly.

2. Create a Dedicated Account: To prevent accidental spending, open a separate savings account specifically for your emergency fund. Make sure it's easily accessible, such as a savings account or a money market account, to allow quick withdrawals when needed.

3. Build Consistently: Start by setting aside a small amount of money from each paycheck until you reach your desired fund size. It's essential to be consistent in your contributions to steadily grow your emergency fund.

4. Keep It Liquid: Your emergency fund should be in liquid assets, such as cash or easily accessible savings. While it's wise to invest the rest of your money, your emergency fund must remain safe and available on short notice.

Mitigating the Impact of Unexpected Financial Challenges

No matter how well-prepared you are, life can still throw unexpected challenges your way. Here are practical steps to mitigate their impact:

1. Regularly Review Your Insurance: Periodically assess your insurance policies to ensure they align with your current needs and life circumstances. As your family grows, your assets change, or your health situation evolves, your insurance should adapt accordingly.

2. Keep Your Emergency Fund Topped Up: If you ever dip into your emergency fund, make it a priority to replenish it as soon as possible. An insufficient emergency fund can leave you vulnerable to future financial shocks.

3. Maintain Good Health: While you can't predict all health-related challenges, maintaining a healthy lifestyle can reduce your risk of illness and injuries. Regular exercise, a balanced diet, and preventive healthcare can go a long way in minimizing unexpected medical expenses.

4. Practice Safe Driving and Home Maintenance: Preventing accidents and disasters is always better than dealing with their aftermath. Safe driving and proper home maintenance can help you avoid situations that might trigger insurance claims.

5. Diversify Your Income Sources: Having multiple income streams, such as investments, a side business, or freelancing, can provide financial stability and reduce your dependence on a single source of income.

Insurance and contingency planning are critical components of your financial security strategy. They provide protection against the unexpected and ensure that your wealth-building efforts remain on track, even when life takes an unforeseen turn. By maintaining the right insurance coverage and a well-funded emergency fund, you'll be well-prepared to face life's uncertainties while continuing to focus on your financial goals.

Chapter 6: Real Estate and Property Investment

6.1 Real Estate as an Investment: Exploring Opportunities

When it comes to building wealth and securing your financial future, real estate is often an attractive avenue to explore. It's not merely about owning a physical property, but rather an investment strategy that can provide a range of benefits and opportunities. In this section, we'll dissect the world of real estate investment, examining its benefits, risks, and the strategies that can lead to a successful real estate portfolio.

Exploring Real Estate Investment Options

Real estate investment encompasses various avenues, each with its unique characteristics and potential returns. To navigate this realm effectively, you must first understand the different options available:

1. Residential Real Estate: This is perhaps the most common entry point for budding real estate investors. Residential properties include single-family homes, condos, duplexes, and apartment buildings. Investing in residential real estate provides a steady stream of rental income, and it allows for diversification by owning multiple units or properties. These investments tend to be less volatile than other forms of real estate.

2. Commercial Real Estate: On the flip side, we have commercial real estate, which includes office buildings,

retail spaces, and industrial properties. These investments often involve longer leases and more substantial rental income but may also carry higher risk due to economic fluctuations.

3. Real Estate Investment Trusts (REITs): For those who wish to invest in real estate without directly owning property, REITs offer a practical solution. REITs are companies that own, operate, or finance income-producing real estate across various sectors. They trade on stock exchanges, providing liquidity and ease of investment diversification.

4. Real Estate Crowdfunding: A relatively recent innovation, real estate crowdfunding platforms allow investors to participate in real estate projects with a lower capital requirement. This approach democratizes real estate investment by pooling funds from multiple investors to finance properties or developments.

5. Real Estate Partnerships: Partnering with others, such as friends, family, or experienced real estate professionals, can be another avenue for investment. These partnerships can involve joint ventures in purchasing properties, sharing responsibilities, and reaping the rewards together.

The Benefits and Risks of Real Estate Investments
Investing in real estate presents several compelling benefits, making it a favorite among many financial gurus. However, it's essential to grasp both the opportunities and

potential pitfalls before venturing into the world of real estate.

Benefits of Real Estate Investment:

1. Cash Flow: Rental income from real estate properties can provide a reliable and ongoing source of cash flow. These regular payments can be used to cover expenses, pay down mortgages, or reinvest in additional properties.

2. Appreciation: Over time, real estate properties tend to increase in value. This appreciation can build wealth steadily, and you can leverage this equity for further investments or other financial goals.

3. Tax Benefits: Real estate investors enjoy a host of tax advantages. Deductions for mortgage interest, property depreciation, and other expenses can significantly reduce your taxable income.

4. Leverage: Real estate allows for leveraging, which means you can use a relatively small amount of your capital to control a more substantial asset. This magnifies your potential returns.

5. Portfolio Diversification: Real estate provides diversification from traditional stock and bond investments, reducing overall portfolio risk.

Risks of Real Estate Investment:

1. Market Volatility: Real estate markets can experience fluctuations, which can impact property values and rental

income. Economic downturns may lead to reduced demand and declining property values.

2. Property Management: Managing real estate properties can be time-consuming and may require expertise in maintenance, tenant management, and legal compliance.

3. Illiquidity: Real estate investments are typically less liquid than stocks or bonds. Selling a property can take time, and there's no guarantee of finding a buyer at the desired price.

4. Costs and Fees: Acquiring and maintaining real estate involves costs, including property taxes, insurance, maintenance, and real estate agent fees.

5. Market Location: The location of your property can significantly impact its value and rental income potential. Choosing the right market is critical.

Strategies for Successful Real Estate Investment
To succeed in real estate investment, a strategic approach is paramount. Here are some strategies to consider:

1. Research and Due Diligence: Thoroughly research the market and location where you intend to invest. Understand local property values, rental demand, and potential for appreciation.

2. Financing: Consider your financing options. A well-structured mortgage or loan can maximize your returns.

3. Property Selection: Choose properties with strong rental potential and positive cash flow. Analyze the property's condition, market demand, and potential for future growth.

4. Effective Property Management: If you're managing properties, ensure you have efficient systems in place to handle tenant issues, maintenance, and financial reporting.

5. Diversification: Consider diversifying your real estate investments across different property types and markets to reduce risk.

6. Exit Strategy: Plan an exit strategy for your investments. Know when and how you'll sell or transition your real estate assets.

7. Continued Education: Stay informed about the latest real estate trends and market conditions. Education is key to making informed decisions.

Real estate investment offers a pathway to building wealth and financial security. Exploring the various options, understanding the risks and rewards, and implementing well-thought-out strategies can set you on a path to success in the real estate market.

6.2 Rental Properties and Passive Income

Real estate has long been celebrated as a potent wealth-building vehicle, and one of the most attractive facets of real estate investment is the promise of passive income. In this section, we delve into the art of owning and managing rental properties, understanding how to generate a consistent stream of passive income through these investments, and the crucial role of property management in achieving real estate success.

Owning and Managing Rental Properties

The decision to own and manage rental properties is a fundamental step in your journey to wealth through real estate. It involves acquiring physical properties, whether residential or commercial, and renting them out to tenants. This undertaking demands strategic planning and keen attention to detail.

Property Selection: Choosing the right property is paramount. Location, type, and condition are crucial factors. Consider the proximity to amenities, job centers, schools, and public transportation. A well-maintained property in a desirable area often translates to a higher rental income.

Financing and Budgeting: Financing your property investment requires a well-thought-out budget. Down payments, mortgages, property taxes, insurance, and ongoing maintenance costs must be factored in. Keep a meticulous record of your expenses to ensure the investment remains profitable.

Tenant Screening: Your tenants will be the lifeblood of your rental property investment. Screen prospective tenants rigorously to minimize the risk of non-payment and damage. A thorough background check, rental history, and credit assessment can help you select reliable renters.

Property Maintenance: Regular upkeep is essential to maintain the property's value and attractiveness. Promptly address repairs and renovations to keep your tenants satisfied. Happy tenants are more likely to stay longer and take better care of your property.

Generating Passive Income Through Real Estate

Passive income from rental properties is the holy grail of real estate investment. It's the income you receive without active involvement, like a well-oiled money-making machine. To generate and sustain this income stream, consider the following:

Optimal Rent Pricing: Set your rent prices at a competitive yet profitable level. Research the local market and adjust rents in response to market fluctuations. Remember, your rental income should ideally cover your mortgage, taxes, insurance, and maintenance costs while providing a surplus.

Lease Agreements: Leases should clearly outline the terms and expectations for both you and your tenants. Ensure rent collection dates, security deposit rules, and maintenance responsibilities are well-defined to prevent misunderstandings.

Automate Rent Collection: Embrace technology to simplify rent collection. Online payment platforms can make it easier for tenants to pay and ensure you receive payments on time. This streamlines the process and reduces administrative overhead.

Emergency Funds: Building an emergency fund for unexpected property-related expenses is a wise move. These funds act as a buffer, allowing you to address sudden repairs or vacancies without feeling the pinch.

The Role of Property Management in Real Estate Success

Managing rental properties, though lucrative, is not without its challenges. The job can be demanding, especially if you own multiple properties. This is where property management comes into play.

Professional Property Management: Property management companies are well-versed in the nuances of real estate investments. They handle tenant relations, property maintenance, and even legal issues on your behalf. While this service comes at a cost, it can be an excellent investment, freeing you from the day-to-day hassles of property management.

Self-Management: If you opt for self-management, be prepared to dedicate time to your properties. Effective communication, strong organizational skills, and the ability to resolve disputes diplomatically are vital. You'll need to stay informed about landlord-tenant laws in your area and be diligent in managing finances.

Balancing Act: Successful real estate investors understand the need to strike a balance between hands-on involvement and delegating to professionals. Property management companies can help streamline the process, but maintaining an active interest in your investment is crucial.

Rental properties offer an avenue to generate passive income and build wealth over time. Owning and managing such properties can be a rewarding experience, but it also demands dedication and financial prudence. Whether you choose self-management or opt for professional property management, the goal remains the same: to turn your real estate investments into a reliable source of income, inching you closer to your wealth-building objectives.

The road to financial success through real estate is often a pragmatic journey—one that requires a blend of strategic planning, a willingness to adapt, and a commitment to delivering consistent value to your tenants and yourself. Success in real estate is not merely about purchasing properties; it's about skillfully transforming them into revenue streams that enrich your financial future.

6.3 Real Estate Investment Options: Crowdfunding and REITs

In the world of wealth-building and investment, there's a category that's often considered as stable as it is lucrative: real estate. Traditionally, investing in real estate often involved buying physical properties, which could be both capital-intensive and time-consuming. However, in today's ever-changing financial landscape, there are alternative routes to enter the real estate market that don't necessarily require a down payment on a physical property. Real Estate Crowdfunding and Real Estate Investment Trusts (REITs) are two such alternatives, and in this chapter, we'll explore how they work and their benefits.

Real Estate Crowdfunding: Democratising Real Estate Investment

Real estate crowdfunding has emerged as an innovative way for individuals to invest in property without the hefty upfront costs and management hassles that often come with traditional property ownership. This method leverages technology to pool together small investments from a large number of individuals to fund real estate projects. These projects can range from residential and commercial properties to development ventures.

How It Works:

Imagine you're interested in real estate investment, but the thought of purchasing an entire property feels financially out of reach. Real estate crowdfunding platforms act as intermediaries, connecting you with a community of investors who collectively fund a specific project. Here's how it works:

1. Choose a Platform: Begin by selecting a reputable real estate crowdfunding platform. These platforms vary in terms of the types of projects they offer, the minimum investment required, and the level of due diligence conducted.

2. Select a Project: Once you've joined a platform, you can browse and choose from a list of available real estate projects. These could include anything from residential homes to commercial office spaces or even larger development projects.

3. Invest: Decide how much you'd like to invest in a particular project. Most platforms allow relatively low minimum investments, making it accessible for a wide range of investors.

4. Diversify: One key advantage of real estate crowdfunding is that it allows you to diversify your investments across different properties or projects. This reduces the risk associated with putting all your capital into a single property.

5. Earn Returns: As an investor, you'll typically receive returns based on your initial investment and a share of the rental income or capital appreciation. Returns can vary based on the success of the project.

Benefits of Real Estate Crowdfunding:

1. Diversification: As mentioned earlier, real estate crowdfunding allows you to diversify your investment portfolio across various real estate projects. This diversity can help mitigate the risks associated with individual property ownership.

2. Accessibility: Unlike traditional real estate investments, crowdfunding platforms often have lower entry

requirements, enabling a more extensive range of individuals to participate in the real estate market.

3. Reduced Hands-On Involvement: While direct property ownership may involve active property management, real estate crowdfunding allows you to pass on the day-to-day management to professionals, freeing you from these responsibilities.

4. Liquidity: Some crowdfunding platforms provide secondary markets, enabling investors to sell their shares to others if they wish to exit a project before its completion.

5. Transparency: Reputable platforms offer detailed information about each project, including its location, expected returns, and the development team's credentials. This transparency helps investors make informed decisions.

Real Estate Investment Trusts (REITs): The Investment Vehicle for Real Estate

Real Estate Investment Trusts, commonly referred to as REITs, have been around for decades and offer another way to invest in real estate without owning and managing physical properties directly. REITs are companies that own, operate, or finance income-producing real estate in various sectors, such as residential, commercial, or industrial. They allow investors to buy shares in these companies, essentially becoming indirect real estate owners.

How They Work:

1. Variety of REITs: There are various types of REITs, each specializing in a specific sector of the real estate market. For instance, Equity REITs own and manage income-producing real estate properties, while Mortgage REITs focus on financing real estate. Hybrid REITs combine elements of both.

2. Diverse Portfolios: REITs typically hold a diverse portfolio of properties, which can include apartment complexes, shopping malls, office buildings, hotels, and more. This diversification helps spread risk across multiple properties.

3. Dividends and Returns: REITs are required by law to distribute at least 90% of their taxable income to shareholders in the form of dividends. These dividends can be an attractive source of passive income for investors.

4. Liquidity: Investing in REITs is highly liquid. They are traded on major stock exchanges, allowing investors to buy and sell shares as they would with any other publicly traded company.

5. Accessibility: Similar to real estate crowdfunding, investing in REITs doesn't require a substantial upfront investment. They offer a way for individuals to participate in the real estate market with relatively modest capital.

Benefits of REITs:

1. Income Stream: The primary advantage of investing in REITs is the potential for a steady income stream. Thanks

to their dividend distribution requirements, many REITs offer competitive dividend yields.

2. Diversification: REITs provide diversification by holding a range of properties across different sectors. This minimizes the risk associated with investing in a single property or location.

3. Professional Management: You don't have to worry about the day-to-day management of properties, as REITs are managed by experienced professionals.

4. Liquidity and Accessibility: The ability to buy and sell REIT shares on stock exchanges makes them highly liquid and accessible for investors of all levels.

5. Tax Benefits: REITs often offer favorable tax treatment, including the potential for tax-advantaged dividends and tax deferral.

Real estate has long been considered a stable and lucrative investment, but not everyone can or wants to be a landlord or buy a property outright. That's where real estate crowdfunding and REITs come into play. They offer a practical, cost-effective, and accessible means for individuals to invest in real estate without the traditional hassles and capital requirements.

When considering these alternative real estate investment options, it's crucial to conduct thorough research, choose reputable platforms or REITs, and carefully assess your own financial goals and risk tolerance. Both real estate crowdfunding and REITs can be valuable additions to your investment portfolio, offering diversification and the potential for consistent income.

As with any investment, there are risks involved, and it's essential to consult with a financial advisor or conduct your due diligence before making decisions. Real estate, even in its digital form, remains a significant part of many successful investment portfolios, offering an opportunity to profit from the ever-appealing world of real estate.

Chapter 7: Economic Trends and Market Cycles

7.1 Understanding Economic Trends

In the world of personal finance and wealth-building, understanding the dynamics of economic trends is akin to having a compass in an uncharted wilderness. The impact of macroeconomic factors on your financial well-being can be profound, and recognizing economic cycles and trends becomes crucial in your journey toward building and preserving wealth. In this section, we will delve into the often intricate world of economic trends, exploring how they can affect your financial situation and sharing strategies for safeguarding your wealth during economic downturns.

The Impact of Macroeconomic Factors on Wealth

Macroeconomics is the study of large-scale economic phenomena, and its influence on your personal finances cannot be underestimated. It encompasses factors like inflation, interest rates, gross domestic product (GDP), and unemployment rates. Each of these elements has the potential to shape your financial landscape.

Take, for instance, inflation. When the cost of living rises, it erodes the purchasing power of your money. Your dollars don't stretch as far, and the value of your savings diminishes. This is why investment experts often stress the importance of investing in assets that outpace inflation, such as stocks or real estate.

Interest rates are another macroeconomic factor that has a direct impact on your financial choices. When central banks lower interest rates, borrowing becomes cheaper, which can be a boon for individuals looking to finance a home or start a business. On the flip side, when rates rise, the cost of borrowing increases, which can squeeze your budget if you carry a lot of debt.

GDP, in simple terms, represents the economic health of a nation. A thriving economy usually translates into more job opportunities, higher wages, and increased investment returns. Recognizing when your country's GDP is on the upswing can inform your financial decisions.

Unemployment rates, too, are a critical indicator of economic well-being. High unemployment can make it harder to find a job or negotiate a pay raise, which may require you to be more cautious with your spending and savings habits.

Recognizing Economic Cycles and Trends
Economic trends are not linear but rather cyclical, oscillating between periods of expansion and contraction. Recognizing these cycles can help you make more informed financial decisions.

- Expansion: During this phase, the economy grows, jobs are created, and stock markets tend to perform well. It's an ideal time to invest and take on calculated risks.

- Peak: The peak marks the height of the economic expansion. Stock markets may be overvalued, and signs of excess appear. It's a good time to reassess your portfolio and consider taking some profits.

- Contraction: This phase is characterized by economic slowdown, job losses, and declining stock markets. Being cautious during this time and having a financial cushion can be invaluable.

- Trough: At the trough, the economy bottoms out, and stock markets may be undervalued. It's a strategic time to invest for long-term growth.

Understanding these cycles and trends can guide you in making investment decisions that align with the prevailing economic conditions. For example, during a market peak, you might want to rebalance your portfolio to reduce risk. Conversely, during an economic trough, consider increasing your exposure to equities to capture future growth potential.

Strategies for Wealth Preservation During Economic Downturns

It's not a matter of if, but when the next economic downturn will occur. Being prepared can make all the difference. Here are some practical strategies for safeguarding your wealth during economic challenges:

- Emergency Fund: Having a robust emergency fund is your first line of defense. Aim for at least 3-6 months' worth of living expenses stashed away in a readily accessible account.

- Debt Management: Reducing high-interest debt can free up financial resources that you may need during an economic downturn. Consider refinancing or consolidating loans to lower interest rates.

- Diversification: A well-diversified investment portfolio can weather economic storms more effectively. Spread your investments across various asset classes to reduce risk.

- Reevaluate Expenses: In tough times, reassess your spending and identify areas where you can cut back. This can help you preserve cash and remain financially stable.

- Open For Information: Stay informed about economic trends and market conditions. Being proactive and knowledgeable can help you adapt to changing circumstances.

- Professional Guidance: Consider consulting with a financial advisor during challenging economic periods. They can provide expert guidance tailored to your specific situation.

Understanding economic trends and cycles is an essential skill for anyone seeking to build and preserve wealth. Macroeconomic factors, recognizing trends, and implementing sound strategies during economic downturns can significantly impact your financial well-being. While economic trends may be complex, your approach doesn't have to be. By staying informed, being proactive, and adhering to a solid financial plan, you can navigate these fluctuations and work toward achieving your financial goals.

7.2 Investing in Changing Markets

As investors, we navigate through the ever-changing landscape of economic trends and market cycles. The world of finance is a dynamic one, where economic conditions can shift rapidly, and markets can be as volatile as a rollercoaster ride. In this section, we'll explore the essential strategies for adapting to these changes, identifying opportunities within volatile markets, and building resilience in your investment portfolio.

Adapting Investment Strategies to Changing Economic Conditions

In the world of investing, it's often said that the only constant is change. Economic conditions are known to evolve, sometimes gradually, and other times, quite abruptly. To thrive as an investor, it's essential to adapt your strategies to these changes. Here are some key considerations:

1. Economic Indicators:

One of the ways to adapt to changing economic conditions is to keep a close eye on economic indicators. These indicators, such as GDP growth, employment figures, and inflation rates, offer insights into the overall health of the economy. By monitoring them, you can adjust your investments accordingly.

For example, during a period of robust economic growth, you might consider investing more heavily in equities, as strong economic performance typically translates to higher corporate profits and stock prices. Conversely, during economic downturns, you may opt for safer investments, such as bonds, to preserve capital.

2. Diversification:

Diversification is a timeless strategy that remains incredibly relevant when adapting to economic changes. It involves spreading your investments across different asset classes, such as stocks, bonds, real estate, and commodities. The goal is to reduce risk by not putting all your eggs in one basket.

When economic conditions become uncertain, diversification can act as a protective shield for your portfolio. A well-diversified portfolio can help cushion the impact of economic downturns and provide stability when certain asset classes are underperforming.

Identifying Opportunities in Volatile Markets

While market volatility can be unnerving, it also presents opportunities for astute investors. Volatile markets often lead to mispricing of assets, creating openings for those who can identify and capitalize on them. Here's how you can spot and make the most of these opportunities:

1. Value Investing:

Value investing involves searching for stocks or assets that are undervalued compared to their intrinsic worth. During market volatility, stocks may become oversold, causing their prices to dip below their intrinsic value. This is the moment when value investors swoop in to purchase assets at a discount.

It's important to note that value investing requires patience. The assets you invest in may not experience an immediate rebound, but if your analysis is sound, the potential for long-term gains is substantial.

2. Dollar-Cost Averaging:

Dollar-cost averaging is a strategy that involves investing a fixed amount of money at regular intervals, regardless of market conditions. This method is especially effective in volatile markets. When asset prices are low, you'll purchase more units of the asset, and when prices are high, you'll buy fewer units.

Over time, this approach tends to lower the average cost per unit of your investments. It helps mitigate the impact of short-term market fluctuations and can lead to better long-term returns.

Building Resilience in Your Investment Portfolio

As you adapt to economic changes and identify opportunities in volatile markets, it's crucial to ensure that your investment portfolio is resilient. Resilience means that your portfolio can withstand economic shocks and recover from setbacks. Here are some strategies for building resilience:

1. Regular Rebalancing:

Market fluctuations can lead to imbalances in your portfolio. For instance, if equities perform exceptionally well, they might make up a larger portion of your portfolio than you intended. Regularly rebalancing your portfolio— selling assets that have become overweight and buying those that are underrepresented—helps maintain a consistent risk profile.

2. Emergency Fund:

In times of financial uncertainty, having an emergency fund is a lifeline for investors. An emergency fund is a pool of liquid assets, such as cash or cash equivalents, that you can tap into to cover unforeseen expenses without having to liquidate investments at unfavorable times.

Typically, an emergency fund should cover three to six months' worth of living expenses, providing peace of mind during economic downturns.

3. Long-Term Perspective:

Finally, building resilience also involves maintaining a long-term perspective. Economic trends and market cycles are part of the investment landscape, but reacting impulsively to short-term changes can have adverse effects on your portfolio. Keep your financial goals in mind, stay committed to your investment strategy, and remember that a well-diversified portfolio can weather a range of economic conditions over the long haul.

4. Reinvest Dividends:

Reinvesting dividends can help your portfolio grow even during market downturns. The power of compounding works in your favor, reinvesting dividends to purchase more shares when prices are low.

Adapting to changing economic conditions, identifying opportunities in volatile markets, and building resilience in your investment portfolio are all vital components of a successful investment strategy. By staying informed, remaining adaptable, and keeping your long-term objectives in focus, you can navigate the complexities of the financial world with confidence and poise, ultimately working towards your financial goals.

7.3 Global Economic Perspectives

In our interconnected world, understanding global economic perspectives is paramount to navigating the complex and ever-changing landscape of wealth creation. This section delves into the role of global economic trends in your financial journey and provides practical insights into diversifying investments on a global scale. We will also explore effective strategies for confidently navigating international markets.

The Role of Global Economic Trends in Wealth Creation

When it comes to building and preserving wealth, it's crucial to recognize the influence of global economic trends. The world's economies are intricately linked, and events in one corner of the globe can have far-reaching consequences for your investments. Here's how global economic trends impact your wealth creation:

1. Global Markets Affect Your Portfolio: Your investments are not confined to your home country. Even if you primarily invest domestically, your portfolio can be significantly influenced by global events. Economic growth, trade policies, and geopolitical tensions in other countries all ripple through the financial markets.

2. Diversification Across Borders: Diversification is the practice of spreading your investments across various assets to manage risk. On a global scale, diversification extends beyond stocks and bonds to encompass international markets. By investing in assets from different

countries, you reduce the impact of a downturn in one region on your overall portfolio.

3. Currencies and Exchange Rates: Currency exchange rates can significantly affect the value of your international investments. When the value of your home currency rises against another currency, it can lead to a decline in the value of your foreign holdings. Conversely, a weaker home currency can boost the value of your international investments.

4. Investment Opportunities Abroad: Some of the world's fastest-growing companies and industries are not based in your home country. By expanding your investment horizons, you gain access to a broader range of opportunities, which can potentially lead to higher returns.

Diversifying Investments on a Global Scale
Diversification across international markets is a potent strategy for spreading risk and maximizing opportunities. Here's how to go about it:

1. Global Stock and Bond Funds: Consider investing in global stock and bond funds. These funds provide exposure to a wide range of assets from various countries. They're an easy way to diversify without needing to pick individual stocks or bonds.

2. Exchange-Traded Funds (ETFs): ETFs are another excellent tool for global diversification. You can find ETFs that track international stock indices, commodity prices, and even specific industries in different countries.

3. Foreign Currency Accounts: If you're considering international investments, it can be helpful to maintain a foreign currency account. This can allow you to convert and hold foreign currencies for investment purposes, potentially reducing currency exchange costs.

4. Seek Professional Advice: Global investing comes with its own set of complexities, including tax implications and regulatory considerations. It's advisable to consult with a financial advisor or wealth manager who specializes in international investments to ensure you're making informed decisions.

Strategies for Navigating International Markets
Investing in foreign markets requires a certain level of understanding and strategy to make informed choices. Here are practical strategies for confidently navigating international markets:

1. Research and Due Diligence: Before venturing into international investments, it's crucial to conduct thorough research. Familiarize yourself with the political and economic stability of the countries you're interested in. Examine the regulatory environment and tax implications for foreign investors.

2. Currency Risk Management: Be aware of currency risk and its impact on your investments. Consider using currency-hedged investments to mitigate the effects of adverse exchange rate movements.

3. Regional Focus: Instead of attempting to cover the entire globe, you might choose to focus on specific regions or countries that align with your investment objectives. Emerging markets, developed economies, and specific sectors all offer unique opportunities.

4. Monitor and Stay Informed: International investments demand diligent monitoring. Stay informed about global economic and political developments, as these can have a swift impact on your investments.

5. Time Horizon and Risk Tolerance: Assess your investment time horizon and risk tolerance carefully. International investments can be more volatile, so make sure your portfolio aligns with your financial goals and risk preferences.

Understanding global economic trends and navigating international markets are integral parts of your wealth creation strategy. By diversifying your investments on a global scale and employing sound strategies, you can take advantage of opportunities while managing risks. Stay informed, conduct research, and seek professional advice to make confident and informed decisions in the world of international finance.

Chapter 8: Retirement Planning

8.1 The Importance of Retirement Planning

When it comes to securing your financial future, few endeavors are as critical as retirement planning. You may think it's too early to contemplate retirement, especially if you're in your 20s or 30s, but let me assure you that it's never too soon to begin crafting your retirement strategy. This section explores the significance of early retirement planning, the importance of setting clear retirement goals, and the strategies that can help you achieve financial independence.

Why Early Retirement Planning is Crucial

Retirement planning is often one of those topics that many of us put on the back burner. We figure there's time to worry about it later, that the future is a distant horizon, and we have more pressing concerns at hand. This procrastination, however, can be a costly mistake. The earlier you start retirement planning, the more time your money has to work for you.

Consider the power of compound interest, one of the most fundamental concepts in personal finance. It's the engine that can turn a modest sum of money into a substantial nest egg over time. When you start saving and investing for retirement early, your investments have more time to grow, which can make a world of difference.

Let's break it down with an example. Imagine two individuals, Alice and Bob. Alice starts saving for retirement at 25, putting away $5,000 per year in a tax-advantaged retirement account, and she continues this practice until she's 35. After that, she doesn't contribute another dime. Bob, on the other hand, waits until he's 35 to start saving and does so consistently until he's 65, investing the same $5,000 per year.

Assuming a 7% annual return on investment, when Alice and Bob reach 65, who do you think will have more money saved for retirement? Surprisingly, it's Alice, who only saved for ten years in her early twenties. Her early start and the power of compound interest helped her accumulate more wealth than Bob, who saved for three decades. This is the compelling case for why early retirement planning is crucial.

Setting Retirement Goals and Benchmarks

The first step in your retirement planning journey is setting clear, concrete goals. Without specific objectives, it's challenging to create a focused plan. Retirement goals can include various elements, such as the age at which you want to retire, the lifestyle you hope to lead during retirement, and any particular financial milestones you wish to reach.

For instance, you might decide that you want to retire at 60, travel the world, maintain your current standard of living, and have $1 million in your retirement accounts by the time you retire. These goals give you something to aim for and help you tailor your retirement plan to your unique circumstances.

One effective way to set retirement benchmarks is to work backward. Begin by identifying your ideal retirement lifestyle and its associated costs. This includes considering expenses like housing, healthcare, travel, and entertainment. Factor in inflation, as prices are likely to rise over the years. Then, determine the amount of savings you'll need to maintain this lifestyle throughout your retirement.

Divide your retirement savings goal by the number of years you have left until retirement, and you'll have a rough idea of how much you should be saving each year. By breaking your retirement savings target into annual contributions, it becomes a manageable and less daunting task.

Remember that your goals can evolve over time. Life is unpredictable, and your priorities may shift. Nonetheless, having a well-defined retirement vision and concrete goals will serve as a compass to guide your financial decisions.

Strategies for Achieving Financial Independence in Retirement

Retirement planning isn't solely about saving money for the future; it's also about achieving financial independence. This means having the financial means to sustain your desired lifestyle throughout your retirement years without relying on full-time employment.

Here are some key strategies to help you achieve financial independence and reach your retirement goals:

1. Start Early and Automate Your Savings:

- Begin your retirement savings journey as soon as possible. The earlier you start, the less you'll need to save each month to reach your goals. Set up automatic transfers to your retirement accounts to ensure consistency.

2. Maximize Tax-Advantaged Accounts:

- Take full advantage of tax-advantaged retirement accounts such as 401(k)s and IRAs. These accounts offer tax benefits that can significantly boost your savings over time.

3. Diversify Your Investments:

- Diversification is key to managing risk and achieving long-term growth. Consider a mix of stocks, bonds, and other assets in your portfolio to balance risk and return.

4. Increase Your Savings Over Time:

- As your income grows or you eliminate debts, allocate a portion of those financial gains to your retirement savings. Incrementally increase your contributions over the years.

5. Avoid Lifestyle Inflation:

- As your income rises, resist the urge to inflate your lifestyle proportionally. Instead, redirect the extra money into your retirement accounts.

6. Stay Informed and Adapt:

- Keep abreast of changes in the financial markets, tax laws, and investment opportunities. Periodically reassess your retirement plan to ensure it aligns with your evolving goals and circumstances.

7. Consult a Financial Advisor:

- Seeking the guidance of a financial advisor can be invaluable, especially as you near retirement. They can help you fine-tune your plan, optimize your investments, and ensure you're on track to achieve financial independence.

By combining these strategies with a clear understanding of the importance of early retirement planning and well-defined goals, you'll be well on your way to securing your financial future. Achieving financial independence and a comfortable retirement is a journey worth embarking on now, no matter your age or current financial status.

8.2 Choosing Retirement Accounts

Planning for retirement is a critical aspect of securing your financial future. It involves setting aside a portion of your income during your working years to ensure that you can enjoy a comfortable and stress-free retirement. A key component of effective retirement planning is choosing the right retirement accounts and employing tax-efficient strategies to make the most of your savings.

Exploring Retirement Account Options

When it comes to retirement accounts, there are several options to consider, but the most common ones are the 401(k) and the Individual Retirement Account (IRA). Each has its own set of rules, contribution limits, and tax advantages, and the choice you make will depend on your employment situation and personal preferences. (*Note: This type of retirement account available for USA citizens, for other countries, you can search the account which can give you same benefits*)

401(k): A Workplace Retirement Account

The 401(k) is one of the most popular retirement accounts, primarily because it is often offered by employers. This workplace-based retirement account provides you with a tax-advantaged way to save for your retirement. Here's how it works:

- Pre-Tax Contributions: When you contribute to your 401(k), your contributions are made on a pre-tax basis. This means the money you invest in your 401(k) reduces your taxable income for the year, potentially lowering your tax bill.

- Employer Matching: Many employers offer a 401(k) match, which is essentially free money. They contribute to your retirement account based on a percentage of your contributions, up to a certain limit. This match can significantly boost your retirement savings.

- Tax-Deferred Growth: Once your money is in the 401(k), it grows tax-deferred. This means you don't pay taxes on your investment gains until you withdraw the funds during retirement.

- Contribution Limits: The IRS sets annual contribution limits for 401(k) accounts. As of my last knowledge update in 2021, the limit was $19,500 per year for those under 50 and $26,000 for those 50 and older.

IRA: A Personal Retirement Account

The Individual Retirement Account, or IRA, is a retirement savings account that you can open independently. Unlike the 401(k), which is usually sponsored by your employer, anyone with earned income can contribute to an IRA. Here's how an IRA works:

- Tax Benefits: Similar to a 401(k), an IRA offers tax advantages. There are two primary types of IRAs:

traditional and Roth. With a traditional IRA, your contributions are tax-deductible, reducing your taxable income. With a Roth IRA, contributions are made after taxes, but your withdrawals in retirement are tax-free.

- Investment Freedom: IRAs typically offer more investment choices than 401(k)s. You can invest in a wide range of assets, including stocks, bonds, mutual funds, real estate, and more.

- Lower Contribution Limits: As of 2021, the annual contribution limit for IRAs was $6,000 for individuals under 50 and $7,000 for individuals 50 and older.

Maximizing Retirement Contributions

Maximizing your retirement contributions is a smart move, as it accelerates your path to financial security in retirement. Both 401(k)s and IRAs have contribution limits set by the IRS, so it's important to strive to hit those limits if your financial situation allows.

- Employer Match: If you have access to a 401(k) with an employer match, aim to contribute enough to get the full match. This is essentially free money, and you don't want to leave it on the table.

- Consistent Contributions: Make retirement savings a consistent habit. Set up automatic contributions so that a portion of your salary goes directly into your retirement account. This not only ensures you save regularly but also removes the temptation to spend that money elsewhere.

- Catch-Up Contributions: If you're 50 or older, take advantage of catch-up contributions allowed by both 401(k)s and IRAs. These additional contributions can significantly boost your retirement savings.

- Roth IRAs: Consider the advantages of a Roth IRA. While contributions are not tax-deductible, the growth is tax-free, and withdrawals in retirement are not taxed. Roth IRAs can provide valuable tax diversification in retirement, allowing you to choose whether to withdraw from taxable or tax-free accounts.

Tax-Efficient Retirement Savings Strategies
Tax efficiency in retirement planning is about optimizing your investments and withdrawals to minimize your tax liability. Here are some tax-efficient strategies to consider:

- Tax Diversification: Diversify your retirement savings across different types of accounts, including tax-deferred (like traditional 401(k)s and IRAs) and tax-free (like Roth IRAs). This strategy allows you to manage your tax burden in retirement effectively.

- Roth Conversions: If you have a traditional IRA, you can convert it to a Roth IRA. While this incurs taxes in the year of conversion, it can be a tax-efficient move if you anticipate being in a higher tax bracket in retirement.

- Tax-Loss Harvesting: In taxable investment accounts, consider offsetting capital gains with capital losses. This can reduce your overall tax liability when you retire.

- Strategic Withdrawals: When you retire, plan your withdrawals strategically to minimize taxes. Consider factors such as Social Security benefits and the timing of Roth IRA withdrawals to optimize your tax situation.

Choosing the right retirement accounts, maximizing contributions, and employing tax-efficient strategies are crucial steps on your path to a secure retirement. These decisions can have a significant impact on your financial future, so it's essential to educate yourself, seek advice from financial professionals, and regularly reassess your retirement plan to ensure it aligns with your long-term goals and objectives. Remember, when it comes to retirement planning, consistency and strategic thinking can make a world of difference.

8.3 Retirement Income and Withdrawal Strategies

When it comes to retirement, planning is key. You've saved diligently, made sound investment choices, and now you're on the verge of transitioning from the accumulation phase to the distribution phase of your financial journey. It's time to explore strategies for creating a reliable stream of income during your retirement years.

Creating Retirement Income Streams

1. Social Security: One of the cornerstones of your retirement income is Social Security. Before claiming benefits, it's crucial to understand how your decisions

impact your future income. Delaying benefits can result in higher monthly payments, while claiming early can provide immediate income but potentially reduce your overall benefits. Analyze your unique circumstances and consider factors like health, life expectancy, and spousal benefits when making this decision.

2. Pension Plans: If you're fortunate enough to have an employer-sponsored pension plan, you'll need to choose between various payout options. Lump sum or annuity payments? The decision hinges on factors like your risk tolerance and the need for a consistent income stream.

3. Retirement Accounts: Your 401(k) or Individual Retirement Account (IRA) is where your personal savings shine. The '4% Rule' suggests that withdrawing 4% of your retirement savings annually can provide a steady income. However, your individual circumstances may vary. Factors such as your expected retirement duration, investment allocation, and risk tolerance will influence your withdrawal rate.

4. Diversification: Creating a well-diversified investment portfolio is essential for consistent retirement income. Combining assets like stocks, bonds, and real estate can help manage risk while generating returns. Some retirees opt for dividend-paying stocks or bonds for reliable income.

5. Annuities: Annuities are financial products designed to provide guaranteed income. Immediate annuities, for instance, allow you to convert a lump sum into regular payments for life. However, the complexity of annuities,

including fees and limitations, makes them a decision requiring careful consideration.

Avoiding Common Retirement Income Pitfalls

1. Underestimating Expenses: A common pitfall is underestimating how much you'll spend in retirement. Expenses can include healthcare, travel, and even starting new hobbies. It's wise to budget for the unexpected.

2. Overlooking Healthcare Costs: Healthcare expenses tend to rise with age, making it crucial to account for them in your retirement planning. Medicare typically covers a portion of medical costs, but additional insurance or savings may be needed.

3. Failing to Adjust Investments: Your investment portfolio should align with your risk tolerance as you near and enter retirement. Consider shifting towards a more conservative mix to protect your assets.

4. Ignoring Inflation: Inflation erodes the purchasing power of your money over time. Be sure to include inflation in your financial projections and make adjustments accordingly.

5. Delaying Estate Planning: Estate planning is an often-overlooked aspect of retirement. Without proper planning, your assets may not be distributed as you wish. Consult with an estate planning attorney to draft or update essential documents such as wills and trusts.

The transition from saving to spending in retirement is a significant financial shift. Crafting a well-thought-out plan for creating retirement income streams, and avoiding common pitfalls is essential. Your unique circumstances, lifestyle, and goals will guide the choices you make as you embark on this new phase of your financial life. Your retirement is a reflection of the hard work and planning you've undertaken throughout your career, and it's an opportunity to enjoy the fruits of your labor.

Chapter 9: Investment in Human Capital and Networking

9.1 Investing in Yourself

In the realm of personal finance and wealth-building, it's easy to become hyper-focused on investments, stocks, and real estate, all while neglecting the most critical asset of all: yourself. The value of continuous self-improvement cannot be overstated. It is the bedrock upon which all other financial achievements are built. In this section, we'll delve into the importance of investing in yourself, how to develop transferable skills, and effective strategies for personal growth, all in a practical and no-nonsense style.

The Foundation of Wealth: You

When it comes to your financial journey, it's easy to get caught up in the allure of quick-fix investment strategies or the latest get-rich-quick schemes. However, none of these external endeavors can replace the value of investing in yourself. The reality is, you are your most significant asset. Your knowledge, skills, and abilities are the driving forces behind your financial success. So, why is investing in yourself so crucial?

First, continuous self-improvement enhances your earning potential. The job market and business world are ever-competitive, and it's those individuals who adapt and grow with the times that come out on top. Developing new skills and staying updated in your field can lead to salary increases, promotions, or even entirely new career opportunities.

Second, investing in yourself enhances your ability to adapt to changing circumstances. Life is unpredictable, and financial challenges can arise unexpectedly. With a diverse skill set, you're better equipped to navigate these challenges. Whether it's learning a new language, acquiring coding skills, or becoming proficient in project management, your newfound competencies can serve as a financial safety net.

Developing Transferable Skills

When we talk about investing in yourself, we're often referring to developing transferable skills. These are skills that can be applied across various domains, making you a versatile and valuable individual in both professional and personal settings.

One example of a highly transferable skill is effective communication. Being an adept communicator can make a difference in your workplace, your personal relationships, and even in your investment strategies. Clear and persuasive communication is essential when negotiating deals, managing teams, or networking with potential investors. This skill alone can open doors and lead to lucrative opportunities.

Another valuable transferable skill is problem-solving. The ability to analyze complex issues, identify solutions, and make decisions is prized in any context. In your career, it can lead to effective leadership roles or management positions. In your financial endeavors, it can help you identify investment opportunities, assess risks, and devise successful strategies.

As you go to your self-improvement journey, consider the following:

1. Identify Skills in Demand: Research the skills that are currently in high demand in your industry or field. This could involve new technology certifications, management techniques, or even soft skills like emotional intelligence.

2. Structured Learning: Invest in structured learning programs, such as courses, workshops, or even advanced degrees if necessary. Online platforms like Coursera, Udemy, and LinkedIn Learning offer a vast array of courses to choose from.

3. Seek Mentors: Surround yourself with mentors and coaches who can guide you in your self-improvement efforts. They can provide valuable insights, personalized feedback, and accountability.

4. Practice Regularly: Developing skills requires consistent practice. Whether it's public speaking, problem-solving, or negotiation, the more you practice, the more proficient you become.

Strategies for Investing in Personal Growth

Investing in yourself is not a one-time event; it's a lifelong commitment. Here are some strategies to ensure that your personal growth remains a constant focus:

1. Set Clear Goals: Define your self-improvement goals, both short-term and long-term. Be specific about what skills or knowledge you want to acquire and why they are important to your financial success.

2. Time Management: Allocate dedicated time for self-improvement activities. Treat your personal growth as a priority, just like you would with work or other commitments.

3. Track Your Progress: Monitor your development. Keep a journal or use digital tools to record your achievements, skills acquired, and goals met. This not only provides motivation but also allows you to assess your growth over time.

4. Networking: Actively engage with like-minded individuals. Networking is a powerful tool for personal growth as it exposes you to new ideas, perspectives, and opportunities.

5. Stay Informed: Keep up with industry trends and developments. Read books, articles, and attend conferences related to your field. Staying informed is key to remaining competitive.

6. Feedback Loop: Seek feedback from mentors, peers, or colleagues. Constructive criticism can help you identify

areas for improvement and fine-tune your skill development strategy.

The most valuable investment you can make is in yourself. Continuous self-improvement, the development of transferable skills, and a commitment to personal growth are the cornerstones of financial success. By following practical strategies and remaining dedicated to your growth, you'll not only enhance your earning potential but also equip yourself to navigate the ever-changing landscape of personal finance with confidence and agility.

9.2 The Power of Networking

In our ever-connected world, networking has become an indispensable tool for career advancement and wealth creation. It's not just about who you know but how you leverage those connections. Building and nurturing a professional network is an art and a science that can help you unlock doors to opportunities, gain valuable insights, and accelerate your wealth-building journey.

Building and Leveraging a Professional Network

Networking isn't solely about attending social events, collecting business cards, or having a plethora of LinkedIn connections. It's about forming meaningful, mutually beneficial relationships with individuals who can contribute to your personal and professional growth.

* Quality Over Quantity: In the realm of networking, less can indeed be more. It's not about the number of connections you have but the depth of those connections. Focus on building authentic, long-term relationships.

* Setting Clear Intentions: Understand why you're building your network. Is it for career growth, entrepreneurial support, or access to specific knowledge? Being clear about your intentions can help you tailor your networking efforts effectively.

* Active Engagement: Effective networking requires an active and genuine approach. Engage with your network, show interest in their lives, and offer support when needed. It's a two-way street, and you'll reap the benefits by being a valuable connection as well.

Networking for Career Advancement and Business Growth
Successful networking isn't about collecting contacts, but about creating opportunities and value. Here's how to make networking work for your career and financial objectives:

* Leveraging Professional Associations: Joining professional organizations and industry-specific groups can be highly beneficial. These platforms provide opportunities to meet like-minded individuals, stay updated on industry trends, and access exclusive events.

* Mentorship and Guidance: Seek out mentors or advisors within your network who can provide guidance and share their experiences. These relationships can be invaluable in

helping you navigate your career path and make informed financial decisions.

* Collaboration and Partnerships: Explore collaboration opportunities with peers in your network. Collaborative ventures, joint projects, or business partnerships can open doors to new revenue streams and expand your wealth-building options.

Building Social Capital for Wealth Creation
Social capital refers to the value embedded in your social relationships and networks. It's not about what you know but who you know and how you engage with them. Social capital can be a powerful driver in your wealth creation journey:

* Access to Information: Being well-connected allows you to access valuable information and insights. This can include tips on investment opportunities, market trends, or even upcoming job openings.

* Trust and Credibility: A strong professional network can vouch for your credibility and competence. It's often easier to secure opportunities and investments when recommended by a trusted contact.

* Financial Support: In your network, you may find potential investors, co-founders, or individuals willing to back your ventures. Your social capital can help you secure the financial support you need.

In the modern world, the dynamics of networking have expanded beyond traditional in-person meetings. Online platforms like LinkedIn, Twitter, and industry-specific forums offer additional ways to connect and share knowledge. Remember, the strength of your network lies not only in its size but in the relationships you cultivate and nurture.

As you build and leverage your professional network, consider the following:

* Consistency: Networking is not a one-time event but a continuous process. Maintain your relationships even when you don't immediately see a benefit. Opportunities may emerge in the long term.

* Effective Communication: Active listening, clear communication, and providing value to your connections are crucial. Being a resource and helping others in your network fosters goodwill.

* Relevance: Keep your network informed about your goals and objectives. This enables them to connect you with opportunities that align with your aspirations.

* Give First: The principle of reciprocity is essential in networking. Offer assistance and support to your connections, and you're more likely to receive the same in return.

Your network can be a rich source of knowledge, resources, and opportunities that can significantly impact your wealth-building journey. While it may take time to develop, a well-nurtured network can become an invaluable asset as you work towards your financial goals. So, remember, it's not just about who you know, but how you build and leverage those connections that can truly make a difference in your financial success.

Chapter 10: Debt Management and Financial Wellness

10.1 Understanding Debt Types and Management

Debt is a topic that often elicits mixed emotions. On one hand, it can provide opportunities and flexibility, enabling us to make significant investments in our lives, such as purchasing a home or investing in education. On the other hand, debt can quickly become a financial burden, leading to stress, anxiety, and sleepless nights. The key to mastering debt lies in understanding its nuances, differentiating between good and bad debt, and implementing effective management strategies.

Distinguishing Between Good and Bad Debt

Debt can be categorized into two primary types: good debt and bad debt. Distinguishing between the two is essential for making sound financial decisions.

Good Debt:

Good debt is an investment in your financial future. It often has the potential to generate long-term benefits that outweigh the costs. Here are some common examples of good debt:

1. Mortgage Debt: Borrowing to purchase a home is considered good debt. It's an investment in real estate, which tends to appreciate over time. Additionally,

mortgage interest is typically tax-deductible in many countries, further enhancing its financial appeal.

2. Student Loan Debt: Financing higher education can be a form of good debt. Education opens doors to better job opportunities and increased earning potential, which can help you repay the loan over time.

3. Business Debt: Entrepreneurs often take on debt to start or expand a business. If managed wisely, this can lead to increased income and business growth.

4. Investment Debt: Borrowing to invest in assets with the potential for high returns, such as stocks or real estate, can be considered good debt. The returns should ideally surpass the interest rate on the borrowed funds.

Bad Debt:

Bad debt, in contrast, is typically associated with consumer spending, often on depreciating assets or non-essential items. It tends to carry higher interest rates and can quickly become a financial burden. Common examples of bad debt include:

1. Credit Card Debt: Using credit cards for everyday expenses without paying off the balance in full can lead to high-interest debt. It's one of the most common forms of bad debt.

2. High-Interest Personal Loans: Loans with exorbitant interest rates, often offered by payday lenders, are considered bad debt due to the high cost of borrowing.

3. Auto Loans: While auto loans are common, they can become bad debt when the interest rates are high, and the vehicle depreciates rapidly.

4. Retail Store Financing: Financing purchases like electronics or furniture through in-store financing options can lead to bad debt, as the interest rates can be steep.

Understanding the distinction between good and bad debt is crucial for making informed financial decisions. The key is to use good debt to create opportunities for growth and income while avoiding or quickly eliminating bad debt to prevent it from impeding your financial progress.

Strategies for Managing and Reducing Debt

Once you've identified your debt, whether it falls into the good or bad category, it's time to take action to manage and reduce it effectively.

1. Prioritize High-Interest Debt: Begin by addressing high-interest debt, such as credit card balances. These debts accrue interest at a rapid pace, making them the most urgent to tackle.

2. Create a Debt Repayment Plan: Develop a structured debt repayment plan that outlines how you'll pay off each debt. Two common strategies are the debt snowball and debt avalanche methods.

- Debt Snowball: This method involves paying off the smallest debts first. As you eliminate each smaller debt, you gain a sense of accomplishment and motivation to tackle the larger ones.

- Debt Avalanche: In this approach, you focus on paying off the debt with the highest interest rate first. This minimizes the overall interest paid over time.

3. Negotiate Interest Rates: Contact your creditors and explore opportunities to negotiate lower interest rates. Creditors may be willing to work with you if you're in good standing and demonstrate a commitment to repaying your debt.

4. Increase Your Income: Look for opportunities to boost your income, such as taking on a part-time job, freelancing, or selling unused assets. The additional income can be directed toward debt repayment.

5. Cut Unnecessary Expenses: Review your monthly expenses and identify areas where you can cut back. Redirect the money saved toward your debt repayment plan.

6. Create a Budget: Develop a detailed budget to track your income and expenses. A budget helps you allocate funds for debt repayment and ensures you're living within your means.

Debt Consolidation and Refinancing Options

In some cases, consolidating or refinancing your debt can be a smart move to reduce the overall interest you pay and simplify your debt repayment. Here are some options to consider:

Debt Consolidation: This involves combining multiple debts into a single loan with a lower interest rate. Debt consolidation can streamline your payments and reduce the total interest paid. Common methods of debt consolidation include:

- Personal Loans: You can take out a personal loan with a lower interest rate to pay off higher-interest debts.

- Balance Transfer Credit Cards: Some credit cards offer promotional 0% APR periods for balance transfers. Transferring your high-interest credit card balances to one of these cards can save you money on interest.

Refinancing: If you have substantial debts, such as student loans or a mortgage, refinancing can be a viable option. It involves taking out a new loan with better terms to pay off the existing debt. Refinancing may result in lower monthly payments and reduced interest costs.

- Student Loan Refinancing: If you have student loans with high interest rates, refinancing can secure a lower rate, potentially saving you thousands over the life of the loan.

- Mortgage Refinancing: For homeowners, refinancing your mortgage when interest rates are low can lead to lower monthly mortgage payments and reduced long-term interest costs.

However, it's crucial to approach debt consolidation and refinancing with caution. While these strategies can provide relief and cost savings, they should be executed with a solid financial plan in mind. Ensure that you don't fall back into high-interest debt once your existing debts are consolidated or refinanced.

Understanding the nature of your debt, differentiating between good and bad debt, and implementing effective management and reduction strategies are essential steps in achieving financial wellness. Debt management is not solely about reducing your financial obligations; it's about regaining control over your financial future and working toward greater financial security and freedom. By following these strategies, you can take meaningful steps toward achieving your debt management and financial goals.

10.2 Other Strategies for Getting Out of Debt

In the world of personal finance, few challenges are as universally daunting as debt. Whether it's the high-interest credit card balances that seem to hover over your financial well-being or the looming student loans that cast a shadow on your financial future, debt can be a formidable opponent. But take heart—just as it's possible to climb a mountain one step at a time, it's possible to become debt-free using practical, effective strategies. In this section, we'll delve into techniques for becoming debt-free, draw inspiration from real-life case studies of successful debt reduction, and learn how to sidestep the common debt traps and pitfalls that can hinder your progress.

The Debt Lasso Method: A New Perspective on Debt Reduction

The Debt Lasso method is an innovative approach that focuses on harnessing the power of proactive financial management to eliminate debt efficiently. Instead of concentrating solely on the size of the debt or the interest rate, the Debt Lasso method emphasizes creating a dynamic and flexible financial plan that allows you to wrangle your debt effectively. Here's how it works:

1. Debt Assessment:

Begin by assessing all your debts, both large and small. Create a comprehensive list that includes the outstanding balance, interest rates, and minimum monthly payments.

2. Prioritizing Payments:

While still making minimum payments on all your debts, identify one debt to target with additional payments. However, unlike the snowball method, which focuses on the smallest balance, or the avalanche method, which prioritizes the highest interest rate, the Debt Lasso method looks at the debt that's causing you the most financial stress.

3. Establishing a Debt Freedom Account:

Open a separate savings or money market account that will serve as your "Debt Freedom Account." This account will hold the additional payments you make toward your targeted debt.

4. Aggressive Payments:

Commit to making aggressive payments into your Debt Freedom Account by cutting back on non-essential expenses, seeking additional income sources (side hustles, freelancing, or selling items you no longer need), or reallocating funds from other parts of your budget.

5. Regular Assessment:

Periodically reassess your debts and your financial situation. As you make progress, you may find that a different debt is now causing you more stress. At this point, you can "lasso" this new debt by directing your efforts toward it.

6. Celebrate Small Wins:

The Debt Lasso method encourages celebrating small milestones along the way. These could be paying off a credit card or reducing a loan balance significantly.

Celebrations help maintain motivation and track your progress.

7. Repeat the Process:

Continue the cycle of assessing, targeting, and celebrating until all your debts are eliminated.

The Debt Lasso method is about putting the power back into your hands, allowing you to adapt and respond to your financial situation as it evolves. This approach recognizes that the debt causing you the most stress can change over time, and it gives you the flexibility to adjust your strategy accordingly.

Real-Life Success with the Debt Lasso

Let's look at a case study to see how the Debt Lasso method worked for a real individual:

Case Study: Lisa's Debt Freedom Journey

Lisa had a mix of student loans, credit card debt, and a car loan. Instead of following a specific debt reduction method, Lisa decided to tackle the debt that was causing her the most financial stress at any given time. Over three years, she eliminated her high-interest credit card debt, paid off her car loan, and significantly reduced her student loans. The Debt Lasso method gave her the freedom to adapt to her changing financial situation, and the feeling of progress kept her motivated throughout her journey.

By adopting the Debt Lasso method, you can take control of your debt reduction strategy, allowing for flexibility and adaptability while maintaining a clear path to financial freedom. This approach empowers you to address the debt that matters most to you at any given moment, making the journey to a debt-free life not only more manageable but also more motivating.

Chapter 11: Entrepreneurship and Business Growth

11.1 The Entrepreneurial Mindset

In the realm of entrepreneurship, success isn't solely determined by business plans, market analysis, or the brilliance of a product idea. Rather, it's the mindset of the entrepreneur that often becomes the linchpin of achievement. An entrepreneurial mindset is the ignition that sparks innovative ideas, propels ventures forward, and sustains resilience through adversity.

Traits and Characteristics of Successful Entrepreneurs

1. Unwavering Determination: One of the defining traits of successful entrepreneurs is unwavering determination. They are driven by an unshakable commitment to their vision, even in the face of challenges that would deter most. They possess an innate ability to persevere, adapt, and carry on, fueling their path to success.

2. Adaptability and Open-Mindedness: The business landscape is ever-changing, and successful entrepreneurs embrace this reality. They're open to new ideas and quick to adapt. They understand that flexibility, agility, and a willingness to pivot when necessary are key to survival and prosperity.

3. Risk-Taking Propensity: Embracing risk is a cornerstone of entrepreneurship. Successful entrepreneurs understand that calculated risks are part and parcel of the journey.

They weigh the potential for reward against the risk involved and are willing to step into the unknown. It's not a reckless gamble but a calculated leap of faith.

4. Resilience and Grit: The path of entrepreneurship is laden with setbacks and disappointments. However, successful entrepreneurs are equipped with an extraordinary degree of resilience. They view setbacks as valuable lessons, and failure is seen as a stepping stone toward their ultimate goal. They have the tenacity and grit to push forward when the going gets tough.

5. Vision and Innovation: The ability to envision the future and innovate is a hallmark of entrepreneurial success. Entrepreneurs see opportunities where others see obstacles. They have a keen sense of what's possible and are driven to create solutions and disrupt the status quo. Their vision sets them apart and drives their business forward.

6. Customer-Centric Focus: Successful entrepreneurs prioritize their customers' needs and desires. They understand that a loyal customer base is the lifeblood of their business. They build products or services that address real problems and improve the lives of their customers.

Overcoming Fear and Embracing Risk
The entrepreneurial journey is paved with uncertainty, and fear is an ever-present companion. Fear of failure, financial risk, and uncertainty about the future can be paralyzing. Yet, successful entrepreneurs don't let fear dictate their actions.

Instead, they acknowledge fear and understand that it's a natural response to the unknown. It's a survival instinct that kept our ancestors safe. However, the entrepreneurial mindset allows them to channel that fear into motivation. They face fear head-on, analyze the risks, and take calculated actions. They realize that without risk, there can be no reward.

This doesn't mean they make reckless decisions. Successful entrepreneurs conduct thorough research, create backup plans, and consult with mentors or advisors. They mitigate risk as much as possible, but they also recognize that no business endeavor is entirely risk-free.

Nurturing a Growth-Oriented Mindset
Growth is a central theme in the mindset of successful entrepreneurs. A growth-oriented mindset means they view challenges as opportunities to learn and improve. It's the belief that abilities and intelligence can be developed through dedication and hard work.

This mindset is in contrast to a fixed mindset, which believes that qualities like intelligence and talent are static and unchangeable. Entrepreneurs with a growth-oriented mindset understand that skills and knowledge can be cultivated over time. They're avid learners who continually seek self-improvement.

To nurture a growth-oriented mindset, consider the following practices:

1. Embrace Failure as a Learning Opportunity: Rather than fearing failure, see it as an opportunity to learn. When you encounter setbacks, analyze what went wrong and how you can improve. Each failure is a stepping stone toward success.

2. Set Stretch Goals: Establish ambitious yet attainable goals that push your boundaries. This encourages continuous growth and challenges you to strive for excellence.

3. Cultivate a Love for Learning: Successful entrepreneurs are lifelong learners. Read books, attend seminars, take courses, and seek out mentors who can expand your knowledge.

4. Seek Feedback and Adapt: Don't shy away from constructive criticism. Embrace feedback as a tool for growth and improvement.

5. Stay Open to Change: The business landscape evolves rapidly. Be open to change and innovation. Flexibility is key to staying relevant and competitive.

6. Cultivate a Positive Mindset: Positivity and self-belief are essential for maintaining a growth-oriented mindset. Surround yourself with like-minded individuals who inspire and support your journey.

The entrepreneurial mindset is more than a theory; it's the driving force behind many successful ventures. It's a mindset that embraces determination, adaptability, risk-taking, resilience, and growth. While it's not the sole determinant of entrepreneurial success, it's a powerful catalyst that propels individuals toward their goals. So, if you're considering the path of entrepreneurship, remember that the right mindset can be your most valuable asset.

11.2 Starting and Scaling a Business

Starting and scaling a business is a pursuit that can be as challenging as it is rewarding. It's the realm where dreams meet reality, where the rubber hits the road, and where innovation and execution intertwine. In this section, we'll delve into the essential steps for initiating a new business venture, discuss strategies for scaling and expanding that business, and draw insights from the journeys of successful entrepreneurs. So, let's roll up our sleeves and dive into the dynamic world of entrepreneurship.

Steps to Start a New Business

Starting a business is a leap of faith, but it's one that can be grounded in careful planning and execution. Here are the key steps to get you started on your entrepreneurial path:

1. Identify Your Niche: Begin by identifying a niche or market need that your business can address. Conduct thorough market research to understand your target audience's pain points and preferences.

2. Develop a Solid Business Idea: Your business idea should be unique and solve a genuine problem. Clearly

define what your product or service is, who your customers are, and what sets you apart from competitors.

3. Create a Business Plan: A well-crafted business plan serves as your roadmap. It should outline your business goals, strategies, financial projections, and marketing plans. Having a business plan is essential for securing funding and guiding your business's growth.

4. Legal Structure and Registration: Choose a legal structure for your business, such as a sole proprietorship, LLC, or corporation. Register your business with the appropriate government agencies and obtain any necessary licenses or permits.

5. Secure Funding: Determine how you'll finance your business. Options include personal savings, loans, venture capital, or crowdfunding. Your choice will depend on the scale and nature of your business.

6. Build Your Team: As your business grows, you may need to assemble a team. Hire individuals who complement your skills and share your vision. An exceptional team can be a catalyst for success.

7. Create a Brand and Online Presence: Develop a strong brand identity and create an online presence through a website and social media. Your online presence is often the first point of contact with potential customers.

8. Test and Refine Your Offering: Before a full-scale launch, consider a soft launch or beta testing phase. Collect feedback from early users and refine your offering based on their input.

9. Marketing and Sales Strategy: Craft a marketing and sales strategy that aligns with your target audience. Utilize online and offline marketing channels to reach potential customers.

10. Financial Management: Implement effective financial management practices. Monitor your business's financial health, maintain a budget, and manage cash flow diligently.

Strategies for Scaling and Expanding a Business
Once your business is up and running, scaling and expansion become the next frontier. Scaling doesn't mean simply growing in size; it also implies doing so efficiently and sustainably. Here are strategies to help you take your business to the next level:

1. Leverage Technology: Embrace technology to automate and streamline operations. This can include adopting customer relationship management (CRM) software, implementing e-commerce solutions, or optimizing supply chain management systems.

2. Diversify Offerings: Consider expanding your product or service offerings to cater to a broader customer base. Diversification can reduce risk and increase revenue streams.

3. Enter New Markets: Explore opportunities to enter new geographic markets. Expanding your reach can be a viable path to growth.

4. Strategic Partnerships: Form strategic partnerships or collaborations with complementary businesses. These alliances can help you tap into new customer segments or gain access to additional resources.

5. Hire and Delegate: As your business grows, you may need to delegate tasks and hire additional staff. A key to effective delegation is ensuring your team shares your vision and values.

6. Customer Feedback and Adaptation: Continually seek feedback from your customers and adapt your offerings based on their changing needs and preferences. Customer-centric businesses are often more successful in the long run.

7. Marketing and Branding: Refine your marketing and branding strategies as you scale. Maintain a consistent brand identity, and consider expanding your marketing efforts to reach a larger audience.

8. Financial Planning: Manage your finances prudently during expansion. This includes forecasting cash flow, budgeting for growth, and securing financing when necessary.

Lessons from Successful Entrepreneurs
Learning from the experiences of successful entrepreneurs can provide valuable insights and guidance on your journey. Here are some lessons from the trenches:

- Persistence is Key: Successful entrepreneurs often faced multiple setbacks before achieving success. Perseverance through challenges is a common trait among them.

- Adaptability: The ability to adapt to changing market conditions and pivot when needed is crucial. Your initial business plan may evolve over time.

- Customer-Centric Focus: Prioritizing the needs and satisfaction of your customers can differentiate you in a competitive market.

- Risk Management: Successful entrepreneurs take calculated risks. They assess the potential rewards and consequences and make informed decisions.

- Network and Mentoring: Building a network of peers and mentors can provide guidance and support when navigating the complexities of entrepreneurship.

The journey of entrepreneurship is not without its challenges, but with careful planning, strategic growth, and a willingness to learn from those who have walked this path before, you can create a thriving business. Remember that entrepreneurship is a continuous learning process, and success is often a result of dedication, adaptability, and unwavering determination.

11.3 Innovation and Business Success

Innovation is the lifeblood of entrepreneurship, driving businesses forward, and setting them apart in an ever-competitive landscape. To be a successful entrepreneur, one must embrace innovation as a core principle, adapt to market disruption, and navigate the waves of technological change. In this section, we explore the pivotal role of innovation in entrepreneurship, strategies for staying ahead amidst market disruptions, and examine case studies of businesses that have thrived by embracing innovative models.

The Role of Innovation in Entrepreneurship

Innovation isn't merely about groundbreaking inventions or cutting-edge technology. It's about finding better ways to address problems, serve customers, and create value. Successful entrepreneurs understand that innovation is a mindset, a commitment to continuous improvement, and a relentless pursuit of better solutions.

Innovation involves staying attuned to market needs, thinking creatively, and being willing to take calculated risks. It's about challenging the status quo, pushing boundaries, and constantly seeking ways to do things differently and more effectively.

Entrepreneurs who prioritize innovation are better equipped to:

- Stay Competitive: In a dynamic business landscape, competition is fierce. To thrive, entrepreneurs must constantly innovate, finding new products, services, or approaches that set them apart.

- Adapt to Change: The business world is ever-evolving, and entrepreneurs who don't innovate risk obsolescence. Innovation equips businesses to adapt to changing customer preferences and market trends.

- Cater to Customer Needs: Innovation helps entrepreneurs understand and meet evolving customer needs. By listening, learning, and adapting, businesses can provide better solutions.

- Drive Growth: Innovative entrepreneurs often experience exponential growth. New ideas, products, or processes can open up previously untapped markets and revenue streams.

Navigating Market Disruption and Technological Change

Market disruption is the byproduct of innovation, and technological change is its catalyst. Entrepreneurs who understand how to navigate these two forces can thrive in uncertain times. Market disruption can come in various forms, including new entrants, changes in customer behavior, economic shifts, or technological advancements. Here's how entrepreneurs can embrace these disruptions:

1. Adaptability: The ability to adapt is a critical skill for entrepreneurs. Whether it's a new competitor entering the market or a shift in consumer preferences, adaptability allows entrepreneurs to pivot swiftly.

2. Embrace Technology: Keeping up with technological change is non-negotiable. Technology can streamline operations, enhance customer experiences, and open new opportunities. Staying informed about the latest tech trends is essential.

3. Know What Market Need: In times of market disruption, it's even more crucial to focus on understanding and what market needs.

4. Collaboration: Collaborate with other businesses or organizations to weather the storm of market disruption. Joint ventures and partnerships can provide new opportunities and resources.

Case Studies of Innovative Business Models
Let's examine some real-world examples of businesses that have harnessed the power of innovation to drive success:

1. Netflix: When Netflix transitioned from a DVD-by-mail service to an on-demand streaming platform, it was a groundbreaking move. This innovation disrupted the traditional entertainment industry, forever changing how we consume media.

2. Tesla: Tesla's innovation goes beyond electric cars. They've transformed the automotive industry by pioneering self-driving technology and solar energy solutions. Elon Musk's visionary approach redefined what's possible in the automotive sector.

3. Airbnb: Airbnb introduced a peer-to-peer marketplace for accommodations, changing the way we think about travel. Their platform not only disrupted the hotel industry but also empowered individuals to become hosts, unleashing a new economic opportunity.

4. Amazon: Amazon continually innovates in various ways, from its logistics and delivery systems to its AI. They have redefined the retail experience and set new standards for e-commerce.

These case studies exemplify how innovation can lead to unparalleled success. By staying ahead of market trends, listening to customers, and daring to do things differently, these companies have not only thrived but reshaped entire industries.

Innovation is the life force of entrepreneurship. It's a mindset, a commitment to progress, and a relentless pursuit of better solutions. To succeed as an entrepreneur, embrace innovation, navigate market disruptions, and adapt to technological change. Learn from the case studies of businesses that have harnessed the power of innovation to achieve remarkable success.

Innovation isn't just about groundbreaking inventions; it's about finding better ways to serve customers and create value. Stay competitive, adapt to change, cater to customer needs, and drive growth through a commitment to innovation. Remember, in the dynamic world of entrepreneurship, innovation isn't optional; it's imperative.

Chapter 12. Wealth Preservation

12.1 Estate Planning and Wealth Transfer

Estate planning is often a topic that many people shy away from or procrastinate, mainly because it involves confronting the inevitable: our own mortality. However, estate planning is not solely about preparing for the end of life; it's also about securing the future well-being of your loved ones and ensuring that your wealth is distributed according to your wishes.

The Significance of Estate Planning

1. Protecting Your Loved Ones: The primary purpose of estate planning is to safeguard the interests of your family and beneficiaries. It ensures that your assets are distributed as you see fit, reducing the potential for disputes and legal battles among family members after your passing.

2. Minimizing Stress and Costs: Without proper estate planning, your loved ones could be burdened with lengthy and expensive legal processes. This includes probate, which can tie up assets and leave your beneficiaries in limbo for an extended period.

3. Control Over Your Legacy: Estate planning gives you the ability to have control over how your assets are distributed and to whom. Whether it's supporting a favorite charity, providing for your children, or safeguarding family heirlooms, you get to decide what happens to your hard-earned wealth.

4. Reducing Tax Liabilities: Proper estate planning can also lead to significant tax savings, as it can help minimize estate taxes and reduce the financial burden on your heirs.

Wills, Trusts, and Inheritance Planning

Wills and trusts are foundational elements of estate planning. They serve as critical tools to outline your wishes for wealth distribution, specify beneficiaries, and manage assets.

A Last Will and Testament is a legal document that provides instructions for how your assets should be distributed upon your death. It's essential for designating guardians for minor children, specifying beneficiaries, and articulating how you want your assets divided. A will is typically processed through probate, a court-supervised legal process, which can be time-consuming and costly.

Trusts, on the other hand, are versatile tools for estate planning. They allow you to transfer assets to a legal entity that holds and manages them according to your instructions. Trusts can be revocable or irrevocable, and they offer a range of benefits, such as avoiding probate, maintaining privacy, and providing for specific needs (e.g., special needs trusts for disabled beneficiaries).

When creating a trust, you designate a trustee, who manages the trust and follows the terms you've outlined in the trust document. The key benefit of a trust is that it can expedite asset distribution, help avoid probate, and maintain control even after your passing.

Minimizing Tax Liabilities in Wealth Transfer

Taxes are an inevitable part of our financial lives, and estate taxes can be significant, potentially reducing the wealth you've accumulated over a lifetime. Proper estate planning can help minimize these tax liabilities and preserve more of your wealth for your beneficiaries.

Here are some strategies to minimize estate taxes:

1. Gift Giving: You can gift a certain amount of money and assets each year without incurring gift taxes. This can help reduce the size of your estate subject to estate taxes.

2. Estate Tax Exemptions: Stay informed about the current estate tax exemptions, which may change over time. Taking advantage of these exemptions can protect a significant portion of your estate from taxes.

3. Irrevocable Life Insurance Trusts (ILITs): These trusts can help exclude the proceeds of your life insurance policies from your taxable estate.

4. Charitable Giving: Consider philanthropic endeavors and include charitable donations in your estate plan. These contributions can provide tax benefits and support causes you care about.

5. Qualified Personal Residence Trusts (QPRTs): QPRTs can reduce the taxable value of your primary residence while allowing you to continue living in it.

6. Family Limited Partnerships (FLPs): These partnerships can be used to consolidate and manage family assets while minimizing estate tax liability.

It's important to note that estate tax laws can change, so it's advisable to work with an experienced estate planning attorney or financial advisor to ensure your plan is up-to-date and optimized for current regulations.

Estate planning is not merely a matter of preparing for the end of life; it's about securing the financial well-being of your loved ones, minimizing stress, and preserving your legacy. With the right combination of wills, trusts, and tax-minimizing strategies, you can create a comprehensive estate plan that protects your wealth and ensures your wishes are fulfilled. Remember that estate planning is an ongoing process, and it's crucial to review and update your plan as your circumstances change over the years.

12.2 Charitable Giving and Social Impact

In the realm of personal finance, we often focus on the pursuit of wealth, financial independence, and securing our future. Yet, there's another side to the equation that can be profoundly rewarding—charitable giving and social impact. It's not just about accumulating wealth; it's about making a difference in the lives of others and in the world at large.

The Benefits of Philanthropy

When you've reached a point in your financial journey where your basic needs and future security are well taken care of, the question naturally arises: what's next? The answer often leads us to philanthropy.

1. A Sense of Purpose:

Charitable giving provides a sense of purpose that goes beyond financial gain. It offers a deeper meaning to your wealth, allowing you to contribute positively to society. It's a way to make a lasting impact, one that extends far beyond your lifetime.

2. Tax Advantages:

Practically speaking, philanthropy offers tax advantages. Most countries provide tax incentives for charitable donations. By strategically giving to causes you care about, you can reduce your taxable income and, consequently, your tax liability. It's a win-win situation where your contributions not only benefit those in need but also your financial bottom line.

3. Emotional and Psychological Benefits:

Research has shown that charitable giving triggers the release of endorphins, the "feel-good" chemicals in our brains. It promotes a sense of happiness, fulfillment, and even reduced stress levels. When you make a positive change in someone's life, it can also change your own.

Strategies for Effective Charitable Giving

Effective philanthropy goes beyond just writing checks. To make a genuine impact and maximize your contributions, consider the following strategies:

1. Define Your Mission:

Start by clarifying your philanthropic mission. What causes or issues are close to your heart? Whether it's education, healthcare, poverty alleviation, environmental conservation, or any other cause, having a clear mission will guide your giving and ensure it's aligned with your values.

2. Research and Due Diligence:

Just as you would carefully research investments, do the same with your chosen charitable organizations. Investigate their track record, financial transparency, and efficiency in using donations for their intended purpose. Websites like Charity Navigator, GuideStar, and GiveWell provide valuable insights into the performance of various charities.

3. Develop a Giving Plan:

Plan your giving. Determine how much you'd like to allocate to charitable donations annually. This not only helps you manage your finances but also ensures you have a consistent impact. Budgeting for giving is just as crucial as budgeting for any other aspect of your financial life.

4. Consider Non-Financial Contributions:

While financial contributions are vital, don't overlook the value of your time, skills, and expertise. Volunteering your time or sharing your professional skills with a nonprofit can be just as impactful. Your expertise can help organizations run more efficiently, making every dollar count.

Creating a Positive Social Impact with Your Wealth
Your wealth can be a force for good, and how you use it can shape the world. Here are some key principles to remember when aiming to create a positive social impact:

1. Be Proactive:

Don't wait until you've amassed enormous wealth to start giving back. You can start making a difference right now, even with modest resources. As you grow financially, your contributions can also grow, allowing your impact to scale.

2. Leverage Your Network:

Your connections can be a powerful tool for philanthropy. Engage your network, including family, friends, and colleagues, in your charitable efforts. Collaborate on projects, raise awareness, and pool resources for a more substantial impact.

3. Measure and Adapt:

Just as you track your financial investments, monitor the outcomes of your charitable investments. Assess the effectiveness of the organizations you support, the progress they make, and the changes they create. If an approach is not yielding the expected results, don't hesitate to adapt and find more effective avenues for making a difference.

4. Long-Term Thinking:

Philanthropy is not a one-time act; it's an ongoing commitment. Consider creating a legacy by including charitable giving in your estate plan. This ensures that your values and your desire to make a difference continue long after you're gone.

Your wealth is not solely a reflection of your financial success; it's a tool that can be used to positively impact the world. Philanthropy offers the opportunity to find deeper purpose, reduce your tax burden, and experience the emotional rewards of giving back. It's not just about accumulating wealth but sharing it for the greater good. By defining your mission, conducting due diligence, and implementing a giving plan, you can effectively channel your resources to create a positive social impact, leaving a lasting legacy of compassion and change.

12.3 Legacy and Wealth Succession

For many individuals and families, achieving wealth is not just about personal financial success. It's also about leaving a lasting legacy and securing the financial well-being of future generations. Wealth succession planning plays a pivotal role in achieving these aspirations.

Planning for Future Generations

Successful wealth succession begins with a comprehensive plan. The goal is not just to pass on financial assets but also values, knowledge, and a sense of responsibility. Here's how you can begin planning for the next generation:

1. Start Early: Wealth succession planning should commence long before it's needed. The earlier you start, the more time you have to develop a well-thought-out strategy. This includes establishing trusts, wills, and estate planning tools that align with your long-term objectives.

2. Define Your Goals: Clearly articulate your objectives for wealth succession. Do you want to provide for your children's education, ensure a comfortable retirement, or support charitable causes? Understanding your goals will guide your planning efforts.

3. Educate and Communicate: Education is key. Take the time to educate your heirs about financial matters, investments, and the values that underpin your family's wealth. Encourage open and honest communication within the family, fostering an environment where questions are welcomed.

4. Legal Structures: Consider establishing trusts and other legal structures that protect and manage your assets according to your wishes. Trusts can be used to pass assets to beneficiaries, protect family wealth, and minimize estate tax liabilities.

5. Professional Guidance: Seek the expertise of financial advisors, estate planning attorneys, and accountants. They can provide invaluable insight into tax-efficient strategies, asset protection, and the legal aspects of wealth succession.

6. Update Your Plan: Life is ever-changing, so your wealth succession plan should be adaptable. Regularly review and update your estate plan and legal documents to reflect new circumstances, changing family dynamics, and evolving financial goals.

Sustaining Family Wealth and Values
Wealth succession is not solely about financial assets; it's also about preserving family values and principles. Here are some ways to ensure the continuation of these core values:

1. Family Mission Statement: Consider creating a family mission statement that outlines your family's core values,

philanthropic goals, and vision for the future. This document can serve as a guiding light for current and future generations.

2. Mentorship and Guidance: Designate mentors within the family who can provide guidance and support to younger generations. This helps instill the knowledge and values that have been integral to your family's success.

3. Philanthropy and Giving Back: Encourage a sense of responsibility and stewardship by involving family members in charitable endeavors. Philanthropy can be a powerful tool for teaching the value of giving back and making a positive impact on the world.

4. Family Meetings: Regular family meetings can provide a forum for discussing financial matters, sharing updates on the family's wealth, and addressing concerns or questions. Open and transparent communication is key.

5. Wealth Education: Promote financial literacy and education among younger family members. Workshops, seminars, and financial discussions can help prepare them for the responsibilities that come with inheriting wealth.

Case Studies of Successful Wealth Succession
Real-life examples of successful wealth succession can provide invaluable insights into the practical application of these principles. Let's examine two such cases:

Case Study 1: The Johnson Family

The Johnson family, owners of a successful manufacturing business, understood the importance of a well-executed wealth succession plan. They began by creating a family mission statement that emphasized the values of hard work, integrity, and community involvement. To educate the next generation, they organized regular family meetings where financial matters were discussed openly. Each heir was encouraged to work within the company to gain practical experience.

Their wealth succession plan included a trust that protected family assets while ensuring that financial resources were available to fund education, business ventures, and philanthropic initiatives. By instilling a sense of responsibility and commitment to their family's legacy, the Johnsons successfully passed on their wealth and values to the next generation.

Case Study 2: The Smith Charitable Foundation

The Smith family established a charitable foundation as part of their wealth succession plan. This foundation not only served as a means to give back to the community but also as a platform for educating younger family members about the importance of philanthropy.

The foundation's board of directors consisted of family members, ensuring that the family's values and vision were at the core of its activities. It provided grants to causes aligned with the family's mission statement, which emphasized social responsibility and community engagement.

By involving younger generations in the foundation's decision-making processes, the Smith family ensured that their wealth was not only preserved but also utilized to make a positive impact on society. The foundation's ongoing success served as a testament to the values passed down through generations.

Wealth succession planning is a multifaceted endeavor that encompasses both financial and non-financial aspects. It requires careful consideration, effective communication, and a commitment to preserving family values and principles. By following these strategies and learning from successful case studies, you can build a legacy that extends beyond financial wealth and leaves a lasting impact for generations to come.

Coclusion: Charting Your Path to Wealth

In the previous chapters, we've explored the intricate landscape of wealth-building. We've ventured into the world of personal finance, investing, risk management, and entrepreneurship. We've armed you with knowledge, strategies, and a roadmap to turn your financial aspirations into realities. As we conclude our journey, I want to leave you with some final thoughts and actions that will solidify your path to wealth.

The Power of Mindset

Achieving wealth isn't solely about money; it's about the mindset that drives your financial decisions. Your thoughts, beliefs, and attitudes towards money play a significant role in your financial success. To chart your path to wealth, it's essential to cultivate a wealth-oriented mindset. Begin by recognizing and challenging any limiting beliefs you may hold about money. Break free from the notion that wealth is unattainable or reserved for a select few.

Instead, embrace the belief that wealth is within your reach, provided you're willing to put in the effort and make smart choices. Understand that wealth is not a destination but a journey. It's about continuous learning, growth, and adaptation. In the ever-changing landscape of personal finance, adaptability is key. Stay open to new opportunities and remain resilient in the face of financial challenges.

The Power of Automation

As you embark on your path to wealth, remember the principle of automation. Automating your finances, whether it's regular contributions to your retirement accounts or investments, minimizes human error and ensures consistency. Automation turns your financial intentions into actions without requiring daily attention.

Consider setting up automatic transfers to your investment accounts, so a portion of your income is allocated for wealth-building before you have a chance to spend it elsewhere. This simple yet powerful habit can make a substantial difference over time.

The Power of Patience

In the age of instant gratification, it's easy to become impatient when working towards a long-term financial goal. But wealth-building is a marathon, not a sprint. Stay patient and remain focused on your objectives. Avoid the temptation to chase quick, high-risk, high-reward investments that promise rapid wealth. Such endeavors often lead to financial setbacks rather than success.

Instead, remember that the key to amassing wealth lies in consistency and long-term thinking. The journey to financial independence may involve ups and downs, but maintaining your course and staying patient will ultimately lead you to your destination.

The Power of Continuous Learning

Wealth-building is not a one-size-fits-all endeavor. It requires ongoing education and learning. Stay committed to expanding your financial knowledge. Understand the different investment options, risk management strategies, and the evolving financial landscape. Knowledge is your greatest ally in making informed decisions that align with your goals.

The Power of Community

Don't underestimate the influence of the people you surround yourself with. Seek a community of like-minded individuals who share your financial aspirations. Engage with mentors, advisors, and peers who can provide guidance, support, and valuable insights.

Consider networking and building connections within your industry or areas of interest. Such connections can open doors to opportunities you might not discover on your own.

The Power of Adaptation

The financial world is dynamic, and your wealth-building strategy should be adaptable to changing circumstances. Economic trends, market cycles, and personal life changes will influence your financial situation. Be ready to adjust your strategy as needed, whether it's reallocating your investments, making career shifts, or rebalancing your portfolio.

Your Personal Roadmap to Wealth

Now, as you stand at the end of this book and the beginning of your wealth-building journey, I encourage you to create your personal roadmap to wealth. Begin by setting specific financial goals, both short-term and long-term. Break these objectives into actionable steps and timetables.

Understand that your journey to wealth is unique. What works for one person may not work for another. Tailor your strategy to your risk tolerance, financial situation, and personal preferences.

Always seek professional advice and expertise when necessary. Consult with financial advisors, tax experts, or investment professionals to ensure that your financial decisions align with your objectives.

Wealth-building is an attainable goal for anyone who is willing to commit, learn, adapt, and take action. The path may be challenging, but it's within your grasp. With the right mindset, strategies, and patience, you can transform your financial dreams into a tangible reality.

Your financial success story is yours to write. It begins with the decision to embark on the journey to wealth, and it continues with each step you take along the way. Remember that the power to shape your financial future lies in your hands. So, go forth with determination, purpose, and the knowledge that the road to wealth is a voyage worth pursuing.

Wishing you every success in your wealth-building endeavors.

BONUS

AFFIRMATION DAILY PRACTICE

Affirmations are powerful tools for changing your mindset and focusing on your goals. Here are some wealth-focused daily affirmation examples along with a daily affirmation menu to help you:

Wealth-Focused Daily Affirmations:

1. "I am a wealth magnet, and prosperity flows into my life effortlessly."

2. "Every day, I am moving closer to financial independence and abundance."

3. "I am worthy of wealth and success, and I embrace the opportunities that come my way."

4. "I attract lucrative opportunities and people who support my financial goals."

5. "Money is a tool that I use wisely to create a better life for myself and others."

6. "I am in control of my financial destiny, and I make smart decisions."

7. "I am open to receiving wealth from multiple sources and channels."

8. "My wealth mindset empowers me to overcome financial challenges."

9. "I am grateful for the wealth and abundance I have, and I share my prosperity with the world."

10. "I trust in my ability to achieve my financial dreams and aspirations."

Daily Affirmation Menu:

Morning Affirmation:

- "Today is a new opportunity for wealth and success. I embrace it with gratitude and enthusiasm."

Midday Affirmation:

- "I am confident in my abilities to make sound financial decisions and seize opportunities."

Evening Affirmation:

- "As I relax and prepare for rest, I reflect on the wealth I've created today and look forward to the prosperity of tomorrow."

Before Financial Decisions:

- "I trust my instincts and intellect to guide me in making the best financial choices."

When Facing Challenges:

- "Challenges are opportunities in disguise. I learn, adapt, and grow through them."

When Celebrating Achievements:

- "I celebrate my financial victories, big and small, with gratitude and humility."

Daily Reflection:

- "Every day, I am one step closer to achieving my wealth and financial goals. I am on the path to success."

INVESTMENT ROADMAP: Turning $5,000 into $1 Million in 15 Years

Year 1 - The Foundation (Age: 30)

1. Goal Setting (Year 1): Define your financial goal of turning $5,000 into $1 million in 15 years. Set clear objectives, including annual milestones.

2. Emergency Fund: Establish an emergency fund with 3-6 months' worth of living expenses. This ensures you won't need to dip into your investments in case of unexpected expenses.

3. Debt Reduction: Pay off high-interest debts, such as credit card debt, to free up funds for investing.

4. Learning Phase: Spend time in Year 1 educating yourself about different investment options, such as stocks, bonds, real estate, and retirement accounts.

Year 2-4 - Early Investment and Diversification

5. Start with a 401(k): Contribute to your employer's 401(k) plan to take advantage of any matching contributions, which is essentially free money.

6. Invest in Low-Cost Index Funds: Allocate a portion of your $5,000 to a diversified portfolio of low-cost index funds, which offer exposure to the entire stock market.

7. Dollar-Cost Averaging: Invest a fixed amount of money (e.g., $200 per month) into your portfolio to benefit from market fluctuations over time.

Year 5-10 - Growth and Expansion

8. Increase Contributions: As your income grows, increase your contributions to your 401(k) and other investment accounts.

9. Consider Individual Stocks: Invest a small portion of your portfolio in individual stocks of companies you believe in. Research and choose stocks with growth potential.

10. Real Estate Investment: Explore opportunities for real estate investment, such as buying rental properties or real estate investment trusts (REITs).

11. Automate Investments: Set up automatic transfers from your bank account to your investment accounts to maintain consistency.

Year 11-15 - Acceleration and Preservation

12. Ramp Up Retirement Savings: Maximize your contributions to retirement accounts, such as a 401(k) or IRA.

13. Rebalance Your Portfolio: Regularly review and rebalance your investment portfolio to ensure it aligns with your goals and risk tolerance.

14. Review and Adjust: Continuously monitor your investments and adjust your strategy as needed. Cut underperforming assets and reallocate funds.

15. Stay Disciplined: Resist the urge to withdraw money from your investments for non-essential purposes. Stay committed to your long-term goal.

Year 15 - Achieving the Goal (Age: 45)

16. Reevaluate Your Portfolio: By this point, your investments should be well-diversified and working for you. Ensure your portfolio is still in line with your risk tolerance and financial goals.

17. Celebrate Success: Once you reach your $1 million goal, celebrate your achievement. Consider your options, such as early retirement or further wealth-building.

Notes:

- Keep in mind that the above roadmap assumes an average annual return of approximately 8-10%, which is a reasonable expectation for a diversified portfolio of investments.

- The specific asset allocation within your portfolio may vary depending on your risk tolerance and investment strategy.

- Regularly consult with a financial advisor to assess your progress and make informed decisions.

This roadmap provides a strategic approach to turning $5,000 into $1 million in 15 years, but remember that all investments carry risks, and past performance is not indicative of future results. Diversification and long-term thinking are key to achieving this goal.

www.ingramcontent.com/pod-product-compliance
Lightning Source LLC
Chambersburg PA
CBHW072157290526
45794CB00004B/1543